33
PROFITABLE
PART-TIME
BUSINESSES

BY THE EDITORS OF

Income
OPPORTUNITIES

PRENTICE HALL
Englewood Cliffs, New Jersey 07632

Prentice-Hall International (UK) Limited, *London*
Prentice-Hall of Australia Pty. Limited, *Sydney*
Prentice-Hall Canada, Inc., *Toronto*
Prentice-Hall Hispanoamericana, S.A., *Mexico*
Prentice-Hall of India Private Limited, *New Delhi*
Prentice-Hall of Japan, Inc., *Tokyo*
Simon & Schuster Asia Pte. Ltd., *Singapore*
Editora Prentice-Hall do Brasil, Ltda., *Rio de Janeiro*

10 9 8 7 6 5 4 3 2 1

Library of Congress Cataloging-in-Publication Data
33 profitable part-time businesses / by the editors and
contributors of Income opportunities.
    p.   cm.
Includes index.
ISBN 0-13-919044-9
   1. Self-employed. 2. Part-time employment. 3. New
business enterprises. I. Income opportunities. II. Title:
Thirty-three profitable part-time businesses.
HD8036.A14 1992   92-20295
658'.041—dc20   CIP

ISBN 0-13-919044-9

PRENTICE HALL
Professional Publishing
Englewood Cliffs, NJ 07632
Simon & Schuster. A Paramount Communications Company

Printed in the United States of America

CONTENTS

ABOUT THIS BOOK

The volume you hold in your hands was compiled, edited, and produced by the editors, staff, and contributors of INCOME OPPORTUNITIES magazine, one of the most respected publications of its kind. Over thirty-five years of experience and research have gone into the making of this publication to help make it, perhaps, one of the most valuable books you have ever purchased.

There is no doubt that you could have learned all that is contained in this book from your own research. But how long would it have taken you . . . months? Years? And how much would it have cost you in time and materials? Far more than the price of this book.

It is far better that you direct your time and energy toward the establishment and building of your new part-time business—and this book is designed to provide you with the ideas and the start-up information you need.

ACKNOWLEDGMENTS

We would like to gratefully acknowledge the contributions of the following authors: William and Wendy Ball, Marsha Chandler, Mike Cummings, Eric Davis, Clare S. Dygert, R.T. Edwards, Sarah Mitchell Gettys, Daniel Hall, Roy Halliday, Bill Hammond, Deborah Stern Harris, Sandra G. Holland, Laurel Holliday, Priscilla Y. Huff, Erik Hyypia, Mildred Jailer, H.K. King, Ingrid Moe Miller, Margaret Opsata, Ellen Paul, Jacquelyn Peake, Troy Robison, Bill Stephenson, Jo Ann M. Unger, and Barbara Vroman; and the following editors: Stephen Wagner, Arthur Blougouras, and Jannean Bryant.

HOW TO USE
THIS BOOK

The format of this book is designed to make it as simple as possible for you to find a part-time business and then put it into operation. It is our intention to eliminate or minimize much of the doubt, confusion, and guesswork that is often involved in any business start-up.

The first three parts of this book provide general start-up information that is applicable for just about any business. The last three parts detail more than thirty suggested part-time businesses based on actual case histories. Before you choose (or adapt) one, read the case histories carefully to get an overall view of the particular business in which you are interested. You'll get a pretty good idea of the costs involved, the work required, the advantages, and the drawbacks—all before you make your first move. When you have chosen an idea, then refer to the basic start-up information. Then you can begin the foundation of your own part-time business.

It is not mandatory that you follow each step exactly as we have presented them here; they are only meant as guides to help you find the easiest, quickest route to success.

Part One:

ESTABLISH
YOUR BUSINESS

You want to start your own part-time business. Whether you need extra cash, are looking for a way to enjoy your retirement, or just want to keep busy away from your regular job, a part-time business of which you are the boss can be a satisfying, profitable venture.

You may have already decided exactly what type of business you are going to start, perhaps based on the suggestions we present in Parts Four, Five, and Six. If you haven't decided, turn to those parts of this book and read about the profitable part-time money-making businesses that others—people very much like you—have started. Perhaps you will emulate one of those ideas, or maybe one of them will spark an original idea all your own.

Are we rushing you? Maybe you bought this book because right now you're just toying with the idea of setting up a business in your spare time. Okay, let's look at some of the advantages a part-time business has to offer.

WORKING PART-TIME

Some people operate businesses at nights or on weekends with the intention of expanding them to full-time operations once they have proved to be profitable enough to supplant a full-time job. Others, for the reasons mentioned above or for other reasons, want to keep it part-time. In any case, a part-time business has definite advantages, at the outset, over a full-time operation:

- It gives you the peace of mind that comes with a steady paycheck coming in from your regular job. This assures that you can put food on the table and pay the bills while "experimenting" with your part-time idea.

- It allows you to experiment with several methods of operation and types of promotion until you find the right combination that brings in the clients and yields profits.

- It keeps your investment to a minimum.

- You may find that you never want to operate on a full-time basis, satisfied with the part-time income that your sideline business will generate.

- It allows you to learn about every facet of your business and to make mistakes without devastating consequences.

Most of the businesses profiled in this book can be run on a full-time basis, if that's the direction you ultimately want to go in. But for now, get to know the business, learn all the ins and outs, and experiment with various operational techniques and promotion strategies. Take your time. Your growing profits will tell you when it's time to go full-time, if that's what you want.

WHICH BUSINESS IS BEST FOR YOU?

One of the keys to the success of your part-time business is knowing which one is right for you to start in the first place. It is vital to determine which business interests you the most—one you'll enjoy working at—and fits your particular background and experience. Remember, a business that is potentially profitable does not mean that it will fit your personal needs or that you will like it.

Many entrepreneurs seek advice from friends and relatives. The problem with this approach is that if you ask ten different people, you'll get ten different answers. Eight will give you different ideas that "can't lose," and the other two will think you're totally crazy for wanting your own business at all.

Here are fifteen criteria for your proposed business that you should consider as they may relate to your personality, background, habits, and your likes and dislikes. If you have not yet chosen any business for consideration, return to this section when you have. If you are trying to decide among two or more businesses, see which one ranks best against these criteria:

1. **Income Potential.** Can the prospective business produce the amount of part-time income you want? The first consideration you should make is how much money you *want* to earn, not what you need. If a business is providing only enough income to provide for your needs and not your wants, you won't be satisfied. If the majority of your competitors don't make the kind of income you hope to make, don't assume that your operation will be that much better.

2. **Sales Calls.** If you don't enjoy making sales calls, don't consider a business that requires you to be an aggressive salesperson. Many people don't know their true feelings with respect to sales calls. If this is true for you, take a part-time or evening job in which you have to make sales calls. You will find out rather quickly if this is for you. All businesses require you to sell,

in one way or another. Selling via mail order requires no personal contact, while direct selling requires lots of one-on-one contact.

3. **Morning or Night Person.** Do you greet the early morning with energy and enthusiasm? Or do you hate getting up early? If the latter is true, you should avoid businesses which may require you to be up and alert far earlier than your clients. It is very important to fit the hours of the business to your built-in body clock rather than vice-versa. If you must totally change your lifestyle, the chances are that in time you will grow to resent and even hate what you are doing.

4. **Travel.** Do you enjoy travel or are you a "homebody"? A part-time business that takes you away from home in the evenings or every weekend cannot be successfully operated by a person who loves to stay near home and family.

5. **Employees.** Most part-time businesses don't require employees other than yourself, but some do. Running a business that requires managing an assistant or two necessitates more effort than a business that only you and perhaps your spouse operate.

6. **Nights and Weekends.** Does the prospective business require that you work both nights *and* weekends? If you are used to recreation and outings with family and friends each weekend, you may resent putting all of this time into your new endeavor. Some businesses (like flea mar-

kets) make most of their money on weekends. Are you ready to make this kind of commitment?

7. **Status.** What are your feelings about your own status in the community? If status is important to you, does your new enterprise afford this status? Does it detract from it?

8. **Family Working with You.** Are you planning to have your family assist you? Do they support the idea and are they willing? The time to discuss this aspect of your planning is *before* you make a change, not after.

9. **Special Training.** Will you need to re-train yourself in order to run your new business? Is the cost and time involved worth the end result? Many people feel that they can't learn new skills or ideas. If this is your feeling, consider only an idea that falls within your current scope of knowledge.

10. **Long Hours.** If you have a regular job, a part-time business may eat up all your spare time. Can you handle this major change in your lifestyle? Can you physically take the greater workload? Will you resent those extra hours?

11. **Future Potential.** Have you examined the full potential of the proposed business? Is the market expanding and increasing for the product or service? Or is it just a fad that may fade away in a few years—or a few months?

12. **Physical Stamina.** Some businesses require a

degree of physical stamina. Do you have any physical ailments which will hamper this?

13. **Dealing with People.** Most businesses require contact with people; after all, it is people who buy your product or service. Some are nice, others not so nice. If you don't like dealing with people, perhaps a mail order operation is better suited to you.

14. **Control Your Own Hours.** Is it important to control your own operational hours? If so, you may not like a business in which your hours are dictated by the convenience of your clients.

15. **Full-Time Potential.** If it is your intention to later expand the business to full-time operation, is the potential really there? Are there enough customers to support a full-time venture? Conversely, is the business *too* time-consuming? Does successful operation demand more time than you can—or are willing—to give it?

THE BUSINESS STRUCTURE

There are essentially three forms of business: the sole proprietorship, the partnership, and the corporation. Most likely, you will be supplying your own money to start your business and so will be operating as a "sole proprietor." But if later you need extra capital, or if the business gets too big for one person to handle, you might consider taking on a partner. It is unlikely that you will incorporate your part-time business.

When that decision does face you, you'll want to be aware of the advantages and disadvantages of each form of doing business. Each has different applications regarding taxes, management, liability of the owner, and distribution of profits. When you do make a decision, you will naturally want to discuss your options with your accountant or your lawyer, but in order to save yourself some time, you will want at least a basic knowledge of the different legal forms of business ownership.

The Sole Proprietorship

As its name implies, a sole proprietorship is owned by one individual. It is the easiest to start and the least complicated to dissolve. If you are a sole proprietor, you have plenty of company: almost three out of four businesses are owned in this manner. And you all share a number of advantages:

1. You own all the profits. No other form of organization allows one person to own 100 percent of the profits earned by the business.

2. Your business is easy and cheap to organize. You don't need any government approval, although you may be required to carry a city, state, or county license. But these customarily involve only paying a few dollars and the simple formality of signing an application. Your only other obligation is to notify your state for the purposes of collecting sales tax, if any.

3. You're the boss. As a sole proprietor, you have

the maximum amount of freedom in managerial decisions. You can expand or condense your business as you see fit; you may sell or close at will; you may change from one kind of business to another, as you wish. In addition, you can make such decisions promptly without having to consult with others.

4. You enjoy certain tax savings. You must pay regular individual taxes on your income, property, and payroll, but these are not levied as special taxes, as with a corporation. You will also have to pay sales tax that you will receive from your customers.

5. You benefit from greater personal incentive and satisfaction. Since you have your investment to lose if your business is not successful, you should be more willing to put time, thought, and energy into the business. And when your business *is* successful, you enjoy maximum sense of accomplishment.

6. You will usually enjoy a better credit standing. Since your creditors can attach your personal wealth, if necessary, they usually will be quicker to extend additional credit to a sole proprietor than to a corporation of equal size and value. The exception would be if you own no other assets beyond your business.

7. You can go out of business more easily. The business automatically ends when you stop doing it, with no legal complications or procedures other than paying off any indebtedness.

As rosy a picture as this paints of the sole proprietorship, there are a few disadvantages:

1. You incur unlimited liability. Practically everything you own is subject to liquidation for the purpose of paying your business debts. If you stop doing business, and your business assets are not enough to offset any debts, your creditors can attach your personal assets to collect.

2. You are limited as to growth. You may have to change to another form of ownership in order to grow as large as you desire.

3. One of the companions to total ownership is total responsibility. You may have to handle some business responsibilities that you have never encountered before.

4. Your business ends with your death or other incapacity. Even though others might attempt to keep the business going, the loss of the individual who started and nourished it will usually result in its closing, even when continued under a new owner.

Don't let these few possible drawbacks deter you, however. For the part-time business, they are not usually factors.

Since you will almost certainly begin as a sole proprietor, you can skip to the next section of this chapter, Name Your Business. The following information about other forms of ownership is provided for possible future reference.

Partnership

Often, the first thought toward changing the form of business occurs when the sole proprietor considers taking on a partner (or partners). The question might come up because you need additional capital, or because a valued employee is no longer content to be just an employee and is thinking of opening his own competing business. So in order to raise the needed money, or to keep from losing that employee, you start thinking "partners."

Like the sole proprietorship, the partnership is easily started, although it is highly recommended that a partnership agreement be drawn up by a lawyer to prevent future misunderstandings. Also, the partnership shares a similar tax situation, but there are additional advantages that pertain to the partnership alone:

1. You have access to a greater amount of capital. Instead of being limited to one person's personal worth, you can double, triple, or even further multiply that capital by taking on additional partners or one wealthy partner.

2. You enjoy a higher credit standing. Like the sole proprietor, a partner's personal wealth is also available to satisfy business debts. But since there are two personal estates available, the partnership will usually seem a much better risk to creditors.

3. You have more than one "brain" to handle management problems. If the partners complement each other, each one suited to different aspects of the business, progress can be accelerated by

their combined, increased knowledge and ability. Also, having someone to consult on business matters can help you make wiser decisions.

Naturally, the partnership form of doing business has its share of disadvantages, many of them similar to the sole proprietorship. Among them are unlimited liability for all partners (regardless of which one makes the bad decisions), growth limited to the amount of capital the partners can raise, and automatic dissolution of the business in the event of the death or incapacitation of one of the partners.

But perhaps the biggest drawback to partnerships is the susceptibility of the partners to disagreements over basic business policies. Even if these disagreements do not cause the business to close, bad feelings can make daily operation difficult for everyone concerned. To have any chance at success, partners must be compatible and seeking a common goal.

The Corporation

The third business structure commonly employed by small business is the corporation, a legal entity with the rights, duties, and powers of a person. As its owners change, the corporation keeps the same identity. Although commonly associated with huge conglomerates, a business doesn't have to be a large organization to incorporate. There are, in fact, many small business corporations. But like other forms of business, the corporation has its own advantages and disadvantages:

1. You risk only the money you invest in the corporation.
2. There is no limit to your growth potential.
3. You can easily transfer ownership.
4. Your business can go on indefinitely.

On the other hand, there are definite disadvantages to
incorporating, including: heavier taxes; higher initial investment; many government restrictions and reports.

NAME YOUR BUSINESS

The importance of the name of a new company cannot be
overlooked, but surprisingly, it often is. The name that you
give to your new business can significantly affect the
business's chances of success. You must be able to distance
yourself enough from what you're naming to find out how
your customers perceive your business, what they want
from it, and what it can do to fill the needs they believe
they have. Try to be ever-conscious of your customers'
demands; let the name of your company serve your
customers, as well as instill confidence in them.

To begin the process, gather a pool of information
concerning your company. First, describe what you are
naming. What services will your business provide? Whom
do you want your name to appeal to? Make a list of the
names that you like and dislike. Use this list as a reference
guide, and explain what appeals to you about your favorites, and what repels you from liking other names. Write
down your competitors' names, and see where they fit onto
your list. Can your business's name compete with others?

After you have gathered some pertinent information, then you can start toying with some ideas for the name of your business. Keep in mind that there are still many things to consider when naming a company that you might not ordinarily have contemplated. Here are five hints which concern the naming of a new company:

1. Avoid initials. A company name like AAA HANDYMAN SERVICE lacks personality and is easily ignored by potential customers.

2. Avoid names that resemble the names of larger corporations. For example, for your photo button business, avoid MR. BUTTON PHOTO BUTTONS since Mr. Button is the trademarked name of a manufacturer of button-making machines. You're likely to find a lawsuit on your hands.

3. Avoid the timeworn and hackneyed word "Enterprises." Look in any telephone directory and you will discover hundreds of firms with names like DOE ENTERPRISES or JD ENTERPRISES.

4. Avoid using your family name in the name of the firm. A family name usually implies smallness, and even though you *are* a part-time business it may not be in the best interest of your image to broadcast that fact. There are many exceptions to this rule, but it is still usually sound advice.

5. Give a sense of balance and rhythm to the name of your company. Avoid long-winded, obscure, or complicated names.

Selecting a name is a very personal and creative activity; you are the one who has to live with the name you choose. It's your money that will promote it and build its reputation, and it's your name that will be associated with it. A solid name can help give you a head start. A clever name is a form of free advertising. A stodgy name will forever be a hindrance to your success.

REGISTER YOUR NAME

The purpose of registering your name is threefold:

1. To record your name so no one else can use it.
2. To receive mail addressed to your company's address or post office box.
3. To be able to cash checks made out to your company name.

Before you go to your county clerk's office to register your name, however, you must decide whether you will use your home address or a post office box. This decision is especially important if you will be offering your service primarily or exclusively by mail order.

Another option is to include both your street address *and* a P.O. box number; in fact, in some states, if you are using a P.O. box, you are *required* to list your street address also. Your street address and P.O. box must be within the same ZIP code. When you list your address like this—

        Acme Aquarium Maintenance
        133 Colonial Street
        P.O. Box 1234
        Anderson, IL 55555

—the mail will be delivered to the P.O. box, yet the customer still has the "visual image" of your solid street address.

If you've decided to use a P.O. box, the annual fee is currently about $30. You will be given a box number and two keys (or a combination). If no boxes are currently available, you will be placed on a waiting list.

With your company name in mind and your mailing address, you are now ready to go to your county clerk's office to register them. You must file a fictitious name certificate if you are using a name other than your own. Even if your name is Jack Wilson and your company name is Wilson's Calligraphy, that is a fictitious name. Only if you were operating under the name Jack Wilson would you be exempt from this step.

The county clerk has a file of all the business trade names in the county, arranged alphabetically either in an index card file or on computer. Call or visit the county clerk's office and tell them you want to register a new business name. They will direct you to the file containing current business names. You simply look in the file to see if there is a business which is currently operating under the name you have chosen. If there is, go to your second choice for a name, and so on. If there are none, you are in luck and you can proceed. The search should take you about fifteen minutes or less. Some offices will conduct the search for you, especially if it's on computer.

The next step is to fill out a few short forms provided by the county clerk. Get the forms notarized (there is often a notary public on the premises), pay the county clerk the registration fee, which ranges from $10 to $100, and you're done. Be sure to get three copies of the forms; you'll need one to open a bank account, one for the state tax department, and one for your own records.

In some cases, the above step can be conducted entirely by mail. The county clerk will send you the forms to complete and have notarized, and you return the form with payment so the office can do the search. They'll inform you if the name you have chosen is already in use.

Open a Bank Account

If you have a good, longstanding relationship with a particular bank—one at which you have your personal checking account or savings account, for instance—that is where you should go to open a checking account for your business. Tell one of the bank officers of your intentions. He or she will have you fill out a few conventional forms, will take your new business name and mailing address for the checks and deposit slips, and will also take a small deposit to open the account. Your checks will come within one or two weeks.

Inform the State

For the purposes of remitting sales tax which you collect from your customers, you must file some forms with your state's Department of Taxation and Finance. Write or call them to obtain the form. Fill out the simple form they send, return it, and within a few weeks you will receive a validated Certificate of Authority which allows you to collect sales taxes. The Certificate's I.D. number will typically be your Social Security number. This costs you nothing.

Other Legalities

The FTC rule. If you're selling your product or service via mail order, the only federal department that has jurisdiction over elements of mail order is the Federal Trade Commission (FTC). If your business will be receiving orders from out of your state—which it most certainly will—the FTC requires that you abide by its Mail Order Rule. It states that unless you clearly specify in your ads or catalogs that merchandise will be shipped within a certain frame of time ("allow four to six weeks for delivery"), you must ship the order within thirty days of your receipt of the order. Failure to comply with this rule could result in stiff penalties. You can obtain a copy of the rule and other information by writing to: The Federal Trade Commission, Pennsylvania Avenue at 6th Street N.W., Washington, D.C. 20580.

Zoning. Although zoning is rarely a problem for the small operator, you should check with your county about zoning ordinances. They vary from state to state, and sometimes from county to county. If your business begins to get large, and you're still operating out of your home, large shipments of packages to and from your home may not be tolerated by your zoning laws (or your neighbors). Check it out.

Special rules. Be aware that some states, such as Wisconsin, have special rules for running a mail order operation. Check with your state authorities to be sure you are in compliance with all laws.

Insurance

Does the owner of a part-time business need business

insurance? Yes! Regardless of the size of your business, proper coverage is essential for survival. The value of your operation must be shielded from unexpected calamities. It's difficult to think how a calligraphy service could possibly harm one of your customers, but if someone gets hurt through your weekend limousine service, you could have a lawsuit on your hands. Your property's value must be made safe from both the "Acts of God" and man.

Loss of property. Some losses are defined as "Acts of God," such as lightning striking your limousine. These are what the law "blames" on God. You can't sue Him, obviously, but you can collect from an insurer if you have property coverage. Equally costly losses are the acts of man: arson, vandalism, bombing, malicious mischief, riot, theft, or the negligent act of an employee or stranger. You will most likely be able to punish the wrong-doer and collect your loss by legal means.

Proper value protection. A business, no matter how affluent, cannot afford to cover all of its values and risks against all kinds of losses. You'd be "insurance poor" if you tried. Therefore, when you lose some or much of these dollar values, they must be replaced. The best replacer is a proper protection plan equal to the maximum potential loss.

Your plan. Business property and casualty insurance consists of coverage for property values and liability exposures. Broad property coverage is available in many states. It insures real and personal values. "All-risk" coverage (subject to reasonable exclusions) is better than less costly "named-perils" protection. If it's available in your state, ask for replacement cost instead of actual cash value coverage to recover the greatest amount of your loss.

It's important to buy the biggest deductibles you can afford so you can buy big amounts of protection for the same dollars. Ask your agent to explain the co-insurance clause in a property policy.

About your lawsuit policy: Since needs vary by size and type of business, it is not possible to make specific recommendations. Your agent may say that the market for certain kinds of liability protection is tight, so insist that he get the broadest form in the largest amount with a deductible you can handle. Embellish that plan with an umbrella policy, one that picks up where the other policy leaves off.

How much insurance? What you buy should be determined by what a survey of your business shows. Even if yours is a new operation in your home or garage, ask for an insurance survey. The company writing your homeowner's policy may agree to write a separate policy on the business property and to extend your homeowner's policy's liability portion, for a charge, to the business activities.

Ask if your present auto policy now covers business use of cars. If not, have your agent help you to accommodate your policy to fit these specifications.

SET UP YOUR OFFICE

You're registered and ready to go. Now it's time to set up the office. The descriptions of the specific businesses in Parts Four, Five, and Six will state what equipment you will need, if any, for those businesses. Here we'll cover what you might need in the way of stationery and basic office supplies.

Business Stationery

You may find this hard to believe, but many firms may refuse to do business with you unless you use business stationery. One wholesale supplier relates that he was flooded with orders from one novice which were scribbled on bits and pieces of paper. The addresses were illegible, orders were sent to the wrong people, and complaints began to pour in. After that experience, the wholesaler absolutely refused to do business with any beginners.

You must present a professional image from the start, and this is most easily done with professional-looking stationery—letterhead and envelopes. It's important for contacting suppliers, distributors, wholesalers, and drop shippers, for sending press releases to the media, and for correspondence with customers. It's well worth the small cost and extra effort.

To start you off, you will typically need 500 letterheads, 500 envelopes, and 1,000 business cards imprinted with your name, business name, address, and phone number.

Miscellaneous office supplies include: a rubber stamp for imprinting your company name and address; an endorsement stamp for all of those checks that will be coming in; a binder for holding your sales tax records; and a desk-sized stapler. You most likely have most of these things around the house already, and if you don't, don't go out and spend a lot of money on all of it. Buy what you need as you need it.

Don't be tempted to buy fancy gadgets or expensive machines. Put your cash to better use in promotion and advertising.

The only other requirements are a desk, a small file cabinet, and a small room or a quiet corner in your house or apartment in which to work. You may also need a bookshelf for trade magazines and books.

Part Two:

CREATE A BUSINESS PLAN

WRITE YOUR BUSINESS PLAN

Even though you will be operating your business on a part-time basis, you still expect it to succeed and grow—you still need an overall plan of action. You begin by creating your business plan. Many businesses—large and small—fail because they had no plan. Properly completed, a business plan will provide the guidance needed to handle routine business details, as well as the business's direction for the future. One caution about business plans must be emphasized: the successful business plan must be developed from an unemotional, objective viewpoint, and the more complete it is, the greater the chance you will have of succeeding in your new business. The purposes of a business plan are described below.

Objective Analysis

The complete business plan is the result of a careful and thorough thought process. It answers common questions before the answers are needed. Your plan should tell you what the next step is. Finances will be accounted for, and records will support your quest for expansion financing. Most importantly, your business goals will be achieved.

- *Your business.* The business plan begins with a clear, concise description of your business objectives. Essentially, it is a statement defining how you are going to make money. This portion of the plan should be succinct, but complete enough so that anyone reading it will know what you intend to do, and why it is likely to succeed.

- *Your markets.* How does your business fill a need in the market? What is the size of the total market? What is likely to be your share of that market, and how was this determined? What is unique about your product or service that gives it an edge in the market?

- *Your competition.* Do you have any competition, and how will that affect your business? What advantages do you have over the competition in your market? What advantages does the competition have, and how will you offset these advantages? If other companies have entered this market, why have they succeeded or failed?

- *Your location.* Does location play a role in the success of your part-time business? If so, how? How will you select a location, or why is the location you have chosen suitable?

- *Your management.* Who will manage your business? If more than one person is involved, how will duties and responsibilities be divided? Who makes the final decision when required? What outside services, such as accounting, legal services, or marketing consultants, will be needed to assist management?

- *Use of funds.* If you need outside start-up funds—from a bank or a relative—your source of financial support will want a detailed plan of how the money will be used. This will require a breakdown of equipment, salaries, rents, utilities, raw materials, and advertising.

Financial Information

Financial data is important for more than just obtaining a loan. It is part of your objective analysis. It will determine how much business you must conduct in order to make an acceptable profit. It will identify expenses that might have been overlooked, or make it clear that equipment and services that you initially thought were essential will have to be postponed. An important function of the financial planning is that it gives you a standard by which to measure your success. Comparing expenses, income, and profits to the plan will quickly allow you to identify success, or the need to overhaul the plan.

Some essential parts of the financial portion of the business plan are:

Financial sources. Financial sources refer not only to banks and investors, but also to your personal bank account.

Equipment list. Do you have the necessary equipment to carry your business through the initial stages of your plan, and if not, what will be needed? Note that "essential" is the operative word, and is not the same as "ideal." Obtain only the equipment necessary to accomplish the initial goals of your business plan.

Balance sheet. Complete a balance sheet showing assets and liabilities. You will probably be surprised at your own net worth. Properly completed, the balance sheet will show your success and prevent early financial disasters, if maintained on a regular basis.

Break-even analysis. Compare the cost of doing business with the gross receipts. There should be money left over after expenses—including your salary—are accounted for, or you are not making a profit.

Cash-flow analysis. On a month-by-month basis for at least a three-year period, determine all expenses, both known and projected, as well as all income that is projected. After two to three years, there should be a steady increase in the profits.

The business plan is a living document. It should be consulted frequently to ensure that your business plan stays on track. It should also be reviewed and revised as necessary on a regular basis. A business plan can be three pages or 300 pages. It is not the length that counts, but the thought that goes into it.

In the world of fast-paced business, the only truly winning business plan is the one that raises financing without collateral. It sells you and your business. It shows that you have the ability and understanding to make your business work. It also provides a clear road map to success, and this is an important function of the business plan, even if you do not seek venture capital, partnerships, or bank financing. If you have answered all of the questions above, the only question left unanswered is how soon will it succeed.

HOW MUCH MONEY WILL YOU NEED?

The charts on the following pages will help you estimate how much money you'll need to start your part-time business. Fill them in according to your particular circumstances. If you already have a typewriter, for example, you needn't fill in the cost for that item. Fill in only the costs of items you will have to purchase.

Regarding the chart of estimated monthly expenses, the basic estimated monthly cost for each item depends on the size of your anticipated operation. You can best derive these estimates on what you reasonably expect in annual sales. Note that after each monthly estimate a number indicates whether you should double, triple, or quadruple the monthly figure to arrive at an allocation for a start-up period (which averages three months). These are factors suggested by the Small Business Administration.

COST OF SETTING UP YOUR OFFICE

Use the following checklist to lay out your own cost estimates of various aspects of setting up your business, including start-up costs. These are one-time expenses. Add other necessary items.

Furniture, Fixtures, Equipment:
    Special equipment for the business $_____
    _____ $_____
    _____ $_____
    Typewriter $_____
    Storage shelves $_____
    Desk and chair $_____
    File cabinet $_____
    Safe or strongbox $_____
    Other furniture, fixtures, equipment $_____
Decorating and remodeling costs:
    Starting inventory $_____
    Deposits with public utilities $_____
    Legal and other professional fees $_____
    Licenses and permits $_____
    Advertising and promotion for opening $_____
    Accounts receivable (money for stock
      until credit customers pay) $_____
    Cash (for unexpected expenses, losses,
      special unforeseen purchases, etc.) $_____

*Total estimated cash needed to set up
  office and start business* $_____

ESTIMATED MONTHLY EXPENSES

The following checklist shows typical items on a cost-of-operation breakdown. Base your monthly estimate on expected annual sales, then multiply by the indicated *factor* to derive an estimate of the amount you will need, as start-up, for each item. Do not hesitate to alter any given factor if there is good reason to do so. Add other items that may be relevant to your business.

	Monthly Cost Estimate		Start-Up Cost Estimate
Salary of owner-manager	$_____	x2	$_____
All other salaries and wages	$_____	x3	$_____
Rent, if any	$_____	x3	$_____
Promotion and advertising	$_____	x3	$_____
Delivery expenses	$_____	x3	$_____
Telephone and fax	$_____	x3	$_____
Other utilities	$_____	x3	$_____
Insurance	$_____	*	$_____
Taxes, including Social Security	$_____	x4	$_____
Interest	$_____	x3	$_____
Maintenance	$_____	x3	$_____
Legal, other professional fees	$_____	x3	$_____
Miscellaneous	$_____	x3	$_____

Total estimated cash needed at start for operational costs $_____

*Payment as required by insurance company.

FINDING START-UP FUNDS

Most part-time businesses can be started with one's own funds. But some are more expensive to begin than others.

For a mobile disc jockey service, for example, you may need extra start-up funding to purchase the necessary stereo equipment and music. If so, don't borrow more than you really need. If you lack the business experience to arrive at a reliable estimate of your financial need (see the previous charts), seek advice from the SBA. Once you have a firm idea about the amount of capital you must acquire, you can better decide where to look.

Check Your Own Resources

Surprisingly, many people seem to be blind to the amount of collateral they have. Perhaps you have invested several thousand dollars in CDs or Savings Bonds over the years, or maybe you own some stock of value. If so, don't rush out to cash them; use them as collateral to obtain a loan from your bank or some other lending institution. You may also have an insurance policy having a cash value against which you can float an alternative or additional loan.

Do you own the house in which you live? If so, you may have money-getting equity. And what about your car? If you own it free and clear, and it is fairly new and in good condition, it may be good as collateral for a few more bucks. But bear this in mind: if you need a different kind of car for your new business—perhaps a mini-van with which to transport equipment and supplies—it might be a good idea to trade the old car in for a new one that will serve both personal and business needs, and only then seek a loan using the car as collateral (provided that you don't buy the new one on installment).

If You Need a Friend

Perhaps you have a friend or a relative who has some extra money tucked away in a savings account, or who owns property that could be used as collateral for a loan. If your business idea is sound, he or she may be more than willing to serve as a financial backer. Don't expect friends or relatives to help you unless you offer something in return to compensate them for the risk they are taking. Your counteroffer may involve nothing more complicated than the written promise to pay them a higher interest rate than they can earn at a bank.

Part Three:

MARKET YOUR SERVICE

Marketing is the most important element of any business because it is all about how to *stay* in business once you've started it. The only way you can make money with whatever business you choose is to: (a) let the public know your service is available; and (b) persuade them to call your service instead of someone else's. This you do through advertising, promotion, and other forms of marketing.

At this stage in the process, you should have already done your market survey, and found out what equipment and supplies you'll need. Maybe you've already got some customers lined up for your service. But you want to get repeat business, and you want your satisfied customers to refer you to additional customers. That takes visibility and credibility, and that's where your marketing efforts come in.

There are several ways to tell your business story to the community: (1) through "free" advertising in the form of publicity; (2) by taking print ads in local media; (3) through direct mail solicitation and handbill distribution; (4) by running special promotions. First, however, the matter of your credibility must be addressed, and to solve that problem you must create a professional image.

CREATE A PROFESSIONAL IMAGE

No matter how hard you work or how in-demand your service is, if you do not convey a professional image to potential customers you are setting yourself up for failure. The part-time business operator who works out of his home, has his five-year-old answer the phone, and uses an off-center rubber stamp to create stationery will have a difficult time projecting an air of professionalism.

There are three vital steps you should take right now if you want to conduct business in a manner that will inspire confidence:

1. *Create a home office.* A home office—a real office in your home set apart from the family room, screaming children, the blare of TVs and stereos, and kitchen noises—can help you to create the appropriate atmosphere in which to conduct your business—even if you never have to invite a client in. Keeping your business materials all in one place will help you protect the continuity of your work.

   If you do not have a spare bedroom or den to use as a home office, you will have to use your imagination. Consider converting your garage, basement, laundry room, walk-in closet, an alcove, or breakfast nook. If all else fails, a corner of your bedroom or living room can be converted into an office with dividers and free-standing shelves. Choose a place that is out of the mainstream of your household, that makes you feel good, one in which you will look forward to working. Wherever it is, make it pleasant. If you will be having clients or visitors, try to choose a location that is close to an entrance.

   You will gain respect, self-confidence, and the opportunity to work more efficiently when you separate the place where you work from the rest of your home.

2. *Install a separate telephone line.* The most important reason for a separate phone line is this: when the phone rings, you know it's a business call. This simple bit of information has many implications. When you answer your business line, you will always use your name or the name of your business which will give you instant credibility. You will have control over who answers the phone and what is said to the caller. For times when you do not want to take business calls, you can install a good quality answering machine or use an answering service.

Your own business line will help further separate your business from your personal life. Your answering machine can insulate your clients from inevitable household disturbances. If the baby is screaming or the dog is barking at the mailman, you can turn on your answering machine and your business phone will be answered in a calm, professional manner.

When your business has its own phone, you will be entitled to a listing in the *Yellow Pages*, and a larger advertisement if you want to pay the additional costs. These are excellent ways to obtain new clients.

3. *Use carefully designed printed materials.* Your business cards, stationery, brochures—all of your printed materials represent you and your business. Quality paper that feels good to the touch combined with an appealing typeface and an exclusive logo will give the recipient an

unspoken message. The first impression that your mailing makes will determine whether or not it is read.

Even though a new business can be short on funds, you cannot afford to skimp on printed materials. Hire a professional artist to design a logo and graphic image for your business. All of your promotional materials should be typeset (or at least done on a good laser printer), and your correspondence should be typed on an office-quality typewriter or printer. Your printed material represents you in the minds of your clients. If you want your business to have instant recognition, create a communications package that will help you convey your professionalism.

Even more than a traditional office-based business, the business operating out of a home must be careful of the image it projects.

HOW TO GET "FREE" PUBLICITY

Public relations (PR) is a highly specialized, sometimes expensive area of marketing. If you paid a PR firm to get stories about your business published in local newspapers and magazines, you would probably wonder just what is meant by "free" publicity. Fortunately, in a small business like yours, it should be a fairly simple matter to become your own press agent. A few simple PR techniques will go a long way toward gaining visibility for your service at a fraction of the cost of conventional advertising.

The first thing you need to do is generate a local-area media list. Get the names of editors of local newspapers, shopper papers (like *PennySaver*), and magazines. Do the same thing with feature editors of local television stations, as well as with hosts of local talk radio and cable TV programs. About two weeks before you formally open for business, notify these people that you're open for business. The most professional way to do this is with a simple press kit, which might contain the following elements:

- A press release that announces the opening of your business, describes what your business does, your hours of operation, your availability, your professionalism, your enthusiasm, etc.

- Photograph of you, the owner, posed at your place of business.

- A one-page press release "bio" that covers something about your background, your enterprising hopes and dreams, and why you started the business.

- A one-paragraph cover letter.

Also include your business card in the press kit for ease of reference. Put the whole package into a simple pocket folder, and send it out first class. You only have to send your "grand opening" press kit to the media one time, although from time to time you may be asked to send the whole package. If this happens some time after you have opened for business, you will want to substitute the "now-open-for-business" announcement for a more current press release. Perhaps you've given a big donation to the United Way, or perhaps you're celebrating your business anniversary. Such newsworthy items will be the lead for the current press release, which you will include in your updated press kit.

Subsequent press releases will usually not include a fancy press-kit pocket folder. Instead, they will consist of the one- or two-page release, business card, and photograph. Generally, you'll have a better chance of getting a story printed if you include photographs; the media like the show-and-tell approach, even if they decide not to run a photo. The photographs themselves should be black-and-white glossy prints or color slides or transparencies. It's best not to send color prints because they are the hardest to duplicate in the printing process.

Some people go all out in their press kits and include something extra in them. If you have the money, you might want to send out an *advertising specialty* of some kind, such as a key chain or an eraser that is imprinted with your company name, phone number, and logo. Advertising specialty companies are listed in the *Yellow Pages*, and sales-people will work with you to choose the item that is most suited to your business. Although this is an extra expense, it is something that you can use as an advertising gimmick for a long period of time. You might want to leave one of your ad specialties with each new client, as a reminder to call for service again.

WRITE A PRESS RELEASE

Local and metro newspapers have discovered that their readers are quite interested in the business activities of persons in their community. Frequently they publish feature stories of local-area businesses. There is no guarantee that a story about your business will get picked up by any publication. To make sure your press material gets top consideration, send out the most professional package you can. In addition to the guidelines above, the following points should help you get coverage:

- Make your copy as informative and as interesting as possible, concentrating on any newsworthy details.
- Keep it short and concise; two paragraphs is about the right length.
- The copy must be neatly typed, error-free, and double-spaced with wide margins.
- On the top left-hand side of the page, be sure to type: FOR IMMEDIATE RELEASE. Underneath that, type the date.
- If you send out your release to a number of media sources, have it professionally photocopied.
- Be sure the release includes all pertinent information, such as the company name and address, plus hours of operation or availability.
- Hire a good photographer to shoot whatever pictures you include with the press kit or with subsequent press releases. Most cities have at least one such photo service. Use the *Yellow Pages* and check around for the best prices. The prints should be glossy, of high contrast, and a minimum of 4" x 5" in size. Business owners who have a media list of several hundred names sometimes keep costs down by ordering four 4" x 5"s printed on a single 8" x 10" sheet, and cutting them later.
- Make yourself available to the media for follow-up questions and explanations. Be prepared to talk about the range of services you offer and any "tips" for readers or viewers on some aspect of your operation or related problems. You should be enthusiastic about the service you're providing.

The release should go out to as many publications as you can afford. Because your service will most likely be concentrated in the local area (although you might be able to market it via mail order, too), this should be no problem for you.

Some people are nervous about writing a press release for the first time. The first step is to look carefully through the newspapers and pick out stories about local businesses. Notice how many of these stories have pictures with them. Collect these stories and photographs over a period of several weeks; you can do this while you're lining up suppliers and other materials for your business. Put these stories in a folder and set them aside for the time being. Now you're ready to assemble your press kit and move on to step two. Take the time to read through the stories about local businesses, and you will find that they present information in pretty much the same way. In fact, you can almost fill in the blanks, from one business to another. Why is this so? Because most of these stories were developed from press kits that were provided by the business owners themselves! Now all you have to do is follow the format of existing stories, adapting the language to fit your particular business.

FROM DIRECT MAIL TO DIRECT CONTACT

Advertising experts agree that you should explore every aspect of free or nearly free forms of publicity, described above, before you spend one dime on advertising. But your part-time business may not lend itself to free press coverage on a regular basis. That's why you'll have to put a more formal advertising program in place. Direct mail is one good way of targeting client prospects in this business.

In direct mail, you send out information about your service in the form of a sales letter, brochure, coupon, or handbill—or any combination thereof. You send these mailings to the names of people on a mailing list. Where do you get this list? Either you compile a list of people who have already used your service, or you rent a mailing list. If you're just starting out, you do not yet have a customer list. So you can rent a list from a list broker.

Be forewarned, however: direct mail may not be a good idea for the beginner on a budget. For one thing, unless you are just sending out inexpensive flyers, it can be quite expensive. First you must buy or rent a list from a qualified broker, then create an attractive, effective mailing piece, and then pay for envelopes and postage. And remember that you can only expect a 2 to 3 percent response rate from such a mailing, even if you confine your mailing to a local neighborhood area.

If you are focusing on the household market, you can rent lists of homeowners and apartment dwellers in specific ZIP codes—sometimes specific neighborhoods within ZIP codes. But because of the costs involved, it is probably best to wait until you have compiled your own list of customers (from sales through newspaper and magazine ads), then periodically send them brochures or handbills that describe your service.

You can rent mailing lists of businesses in specific ZIP codes or industry segments. Again, there are significant minimum costs involved with identifying and targeting the persons who may be in charge of negotiating with services such as yours. On the other hand, you can save money if you start following the new-business listings in your area. You can make a practice of compiling names and addresses of businesspersons to contact as you build your business. When it's time to start marketing your service, you will have a list all ready for mailing.

Once you have a track record, you might want to give direct mail a shot, particularly if you are expanding the scope of your business to include a variety of services beyond your original idea. As we've stated, with the right list, a well-done direct mail package to the right customer list can be quite effective in bringing in new service orders.

Where to Get Mailing Lists

You can find mailing list brokers by looking in your nearest big city *Yellow Pages* under "Advertising—Direct Mail" or "Mailing Lists." A good broker will have access to mailing lists for every possible category of client: home-owner, apartment dweller, apartment managers, plumbing contractors, dentists. Some list names are printed on self-adhesive labels, while others come on computer disks and can be slipped into your PC. Rental prices vary accordingly. Some lists include telephone numbers, and others do not. When you rent a list, you are authorized to use that list only once.

The Direct Mail Piece

Above all, a direct mail piece must be interesting. This is true whether you're sending out a one-page handbill or a five-piece mailing package. Many times, self-mailers (a direct mail piece that is folded and stamped to form its own envelope) or ordinary envelopes addressed to "Resident" look like junk mail for recipients to throw away unopened and unread. If you use self-mailers, therefore, you need to have a "hook" that will persuade the recipient to open and read the material that's inside.

Here are some ways to get the most out of direct mail:

- Enclose reprints of your display ads or articles written about your company.
- Encourage service orders with discount offers.
- Include a deadline notice, such as "Call before May 15."

A self-mailer measuring 8½" x 11" can be printed and trifolded by an offset printing house. Use either card stock or 20-lb. colored paper stock. What's inside the mailer can take many forms: an information piece that announces the availability of your service, a dollars-off coupon, or the equivalent of a big display ad or a handbill. The purpose of the self-mailer is quite simple: to motivate the recipient to call you and place a service order. A self-mailer can also save money on postage.

Using Brochures, Handbills, Coupon Mailers

You will need to have on hand a standard informational brochure that describes the services you offer. The pitch letters you send out to customer prospects will change on a regular basis, and you can have special handbills or coupons printed as they are required. Have an offset printer run 2,000 or so copies of a brochure (trifolded

8½" x 11" or single-folded 7¼" x 8½") that highlights all the services you provide. A little-known way to heighten impact is to use a gray or light blue card stock and an ink like navy or dark magenta. This should cost about the same as boring old black ink and white card stock, but it will be perceived as a professional, two-color piece.

For an initial mailing to commercial clients, write an enthusiastic, one-page pitch letter that introduces your service and asks for business. Mail the letter, brochure, and your business card in a standard #10 envelope to your list of names. After you have been in business for a while, redo your pitch letter in the form of a reminder that you offer competitive services to the business community. You should also develop a standard pitch letter that you send out to new businesses in the community, in which you make the new enterprise aware of your services. A colorful first-class commemorative stamp often improves response rate. If business prospects don't call you, follow up by phone about ten days later to remind them of who you are and what you offer.

Handbills are sometimes considered to be the same as brochures, but the term usually refers to single sheets of paper handed out to passersby or placed on car windshields. Some handbills are produced in the form of door-hangers that are put on doorknobs. Typically, they are inexpensive to produce in large volume at an offset house.

A good handbill has all the features of good direct mail or ad copy, and it may be used to announce everything from a grand opening to a discount promotion. The expensive aspect of handbills is distribution, for you're going to have to pay somebody to put handbills on the windshield or doorknob of every car or front door in a neighborhood. If you can't find some students to distribute your handbills in a neighborhood after school, you might ask your offset printer to refer you to people who distribute handbills for a living.

Another way to distribute handbills is to put them up as notices on community bulletin boards. Often, such boards have restrictions about the kinds of notices that can be placed on them. If you're only allowed to post index cards on a board, then it's worth the effort to get your promotional information printed on some colored index cards. You can place these on boards, automobiles, and front doors, or you can hand them out to customers and ask them to pass the information along to their friends. This can be an effective way of improving word-of-mouth advertising.

Coupon mailers have become popular in many cities in recent years. Coupon-mail advertising, sometimes called cooperative direct mail advertising, is an offshoot of more conventional direct mail advertising. A typical cooperative direct mail package is not personalized but is sent to "Resident" or "Occupant" in a localized market area. It usually includes discount offers from a dozen or so noncompeting local advertisers. Coupons from one car wash, one pizza parlor, one maid service, and so on, will be included in the package. A coupon mailer, which may be one-, two-, or (sometimes) four-color, generally measures 3⅝" x 8½" and fits perfectly into a #10 envelope. Costs for the advertiser are roughly competitive with display advertising.

HOW TO USE CLASSIFIED AND DISPLAY ADS

As a beginner, you may be unsure whether you should begin with an inexpensive classified ad, or take a chance on a more eye-catching display ad. There are reasons for using one or the other.

You use classified ads:

1. When you want to receive inquiries from potential customers, then follow up those inquiries with literature to close the sale.

2. To sell directly from the ad, to persons who are "presold" and who simply want to order a particular service.

You use a display ad:

1. When you want to use a photo, logo, or other illustration to project the professionalism and strong image of your company.

2. When you want to attract attention to your company and receive service-order calls.

3. When your service appeals to a large segment of the target market.

4. When you need the space to tell the complete story of your company's concept.

Classified Ads

Classified advertising is generally recognized as the least expensive way to get news of your service's availability before the market. Virtually all magazines and newspapers that you will be using carry a classified section, and in most communities there will be at least two publications that will be available to sustain an ad campaign. Aside from being low in cost, a classified ad is the easiest to get into print and an inexpensive way to get a great deal of experience in telling your story in the least number of words possible.

You doubtless know what a classified ad looks like; in this trade it is a short-worded message containing a direct, brief statement or "pitch," and a telephone number. Classified ads are published in local bulletins, community newspapers, shopper papers, weekly and daily newspapers, and a variety of magazines.

The price of a classified ad is usually determined by the number of words it contains. Some newspapers with small circulations charge by the line. The large publications that charge on a per-word basis charge anywhere from $1 to $7—or more—per word. The larger the publication's circulation (number of readers), the higher the per-word price. In a local paper with a circulation of 30,000 readers, for example, the word rate would be in the neighborhood of 25¢ to 55¢. This low rate is due to the relative "overhead" costs of keeping that publication alive. In a magazine with a circulation of 300,000 (such as a glossy "city" magazine), word rates may range from $2 to $5 per word. Most include a "minimum rule," such as a minimum of $15 or so many words.

Placing the Ad

Place your ad in the area publications which your target clients are most likely to read. Since you will probably be charged by the word, you will have to learn to write concisely, making every word work hard for the money you are spending. Your name and telephone number will probably amount to four words, so the body copy of your ad will probably consist of another ten to fifteen words. The best classified ads never go beyond twenty words. As an example, here is an ad you might place for a calligraphy service:

> CALLIGRAPHY—Beautiful custom writing for prestigious wedding invitations, special occasions. Fast service. Affordable. Call Erin, 555-5555.

To succeed with a classified ad, you must first gain the attention of the reader. The appeal of your service should be one of four things: what the reader wants to *gain, save, do,* or *be.* The most successful ads lead off by promising to *do* something of benefit to the reader, or to make him want to *gain* more information. This selling technique also applies to display advertising, as we shall see. Experiment with ways to incorporate some informational sale copy into your classified ad. The idea in the above ad is to motivate readers to telephone you. Every name you generate from an ad is one that you can add to your house file. You can either arrange an appointment to submit a proposal over the phone or send the prospect a brochure and then follow up a week later.

Display Ads

Display ads, like classified ads, will be geared toward publications such as newspapers and magazines, and you will undoubtedly find that once you start placing classified ads, the advertising sales departments of various publications will be encouraging you to "trade up" to display advertising. There is even a hybrid form of print advertising known as the "classified display ad." This kind of ad, which is quite common in glossy city magazines, usually includes standard classified copy, plus a simple piece of art such as a logo. But display ads and even classified display ads are not confined to periodicals. The *Yellow Pages*, local TV guides that are available at supermarket checkout counters, and cooperative coupon mailers are all potential outlets for your display advertising efforts. You might find yourself adapting a basic display ad to the needs of a particular medium. As you gain experience in advertising, you will see what alterations in your basic message have to be made.

What is the secret to successful display advertising? It's really no secret at all. All it takes is three things:

1. You've got to offer a service that people want, or at least *think* they want.

2. You've got to know when and where to advertise your service—which magazine or directory to use, which month or day to run your ad.

3. Your ad must motivate people to action.

So far, we've shown you how to achieve or find numbers one and two. Now on to number three.

How to Write Good Ads

First, let us define what we mean by a "good ad." The criterion for a good ad is clear cut. An ad that produces a profit, either by pulling service orders directly, or by getting inquiries that are converted into sales through follow-up literature is a good ad. Results can be measured right down to the last penny, and the results are what count.

Your ad will be competing with dozens of others to attract the attention of the reader. Unless you can get the reader at least to glance at your ad, by attracting his or her attention, your service can be the best within a hundred miles, but you won't sell anything.

Imagine yourself on a railroad track with an express train speeding toward you. You want to tell the engineer that the bridge up ahead is washed out. First you've got to get him to stop. Somehow you must attract his attention. Only after he stops the train can you tell him about the bridge. You pick up a small red flag and begin waving it desperately. Your most eloquent and persuasive description of the bridge is useless unless the engineer stops the train and listens to what you say.

Attract Attention

Your reader is the engineer of the train. He's glancing over the dozens of ads quickly. His eye catches a headline or a picture. He slows the train momentarily, then resumes speed. Now he's coming to your ad. The headline of your ad is your "flag."

So much for the analogy. So how do you attract attention in a display ad? As you will see, there are essentially four basic ways. Each will be discussed in detail:

1. The "angle."

2. The headline.

3. The picture.

4. The layout.

The "Angle"

What is your basic advertising appeal? This is your angle. In short, your angle is what your service can do for your customer. Your prospect has a one-track mind. His or her motivation for buying any service is self-interest. He or she asks one question: "Why would I want to use this service?" Answer this question. Show in words and/or pictures how your service can provide what the customer desires.

Customers want: comfort, convenience; more leisure time; good service; security; new ways of doing things; bargains; enjoyment.

They want to improve their: appearance; self-confidence; personality; status; personal prestige.

Notice that not one of the above qualities has anything specific to do with any particular business. Although you are *selling* a specific service, customers are *buying* convenience, comfort, security, leisure, and status. Sell them the basics—what they need.

The Headline

Use as many words as it takes to attract attention and to offer the angle. Strictly speaking, there is no limit to the number of words in a good headline, although many advertisers have found that the fewer words it takes to attract attention, the better. More important, there *are* key words that can often increase the power of a headline tremendously. Here is a partial list:

absolutely	easy	latest	secret
amazing	exciting	lifetime	sensational
approved	exclusive	lowest	simplified
authentic	fortune	magic	special
bargain	free	miracle	strong
better	genuine	powerful	surprise
complete	gift	profitable	tested
confidential	guaranteed	quality	unique
delivered	improved	rare	valuable
discount	largest	revolutionary	wealth

You may think these words are overworked and lack punch. But repeated tests prove that they out-pull clever, intellectual words by a wide margin.

In a headline, there is probably no word that attracts more attention and public interest than the word "FREE." No other word in the language can do more for your ad. If you can find a way to offer something for free, by all means do so. Consider, for example, offering some free tutoring to a customer who referred your service to five other people.

The Picture

If you have room, use a logo or some other picture that evokes what your service does to help tell your story. Many services that take large *Yellow Pages* ads simply use clip art. Whoever designs your ad, or takes your photographs, is a creative type, and may have some interesting ideas for visuals. Whatever kind of picture you decide to use, it should be easy on the eye, neither too busy nor too obscure for the reader to realize at once the kind of service he's being asked to deal with.

The Layout

On a small two-inch or three-inch display ad, there isn't much you can do about layout. You can arrange line drawings, margins, and type to match the contour of your illustrations, or use a bold border. Don't be afraid to experiment with effective ways of making your layout different from all the others. Notice what competitors do, and try to make your ads at least as exciting as theirs.

Basically, a layout will attract attention in one of two ways, if it is: (1) made dynamically powerful so it dominates the page by its visual impact; (2) made so simple and plain that its sheer restraint, on a page filled with bold, dynamic ads, captures the reader's attention.

Body Copy

Now that you have captured the interest of your readers, you must sell them on your new service. Here's how:

1. Tell about the value and benefits of your service.

2. Prove it.

3. Persuade readers to grasp these benefits.

4. Ask for action.

Your main concern is to include as much valuable information about what your service does as you can, without writing a whole book about it. The trick is to keep your reader interested. Long columns of straight body copy discourage readers. Use subheads and bulleted lists to entice the reader. The subhead is a preview of what's to come. They excite curiosity and boost interest in the lists or other copy that follows.

If possible, run your subheads in sequence, to carry your story in "shots" from beginning to end. Change the size, color, or typeface of subheads to make them stand out from lists or body copy. Use liberal white space around them to create a dynamic, easy-to-read layout.

To write powerful copy, follow these ten basic rules:

1. Use subheads.

2. Use simple, easily understood words.

3. Use short words, short sentences, short paragraphs, but enough words to sell your readers.

4. Write copy as if you were talking to one person, not addressing an audience.

5. Use testimonials—praise from satisfied clients.

6. Include guarantees.

7. Offer a discount or money-back guarantee, if possible.

8. Tell the reader to act, and tell him why he should act *now*.

9. Offer a free gift.

10. Include contact information (such as your phone number) in every ad.

All of the factors that go into display advertising for publications can be applied to coupon-mailer advertising as well. There is one additional factor that most coupon-mailer advertisers take into account, and that is the limited-time element. One reason for sending a coupon to a prospective customer's home is to encourage him or her to take advantage of a special offer of some kind. A $10 discount is a good example, and if it is tied to a reminder that the offer expires on a certain date, so much the better. This encourages the prospect to act *now*.

Study ads for services similar to yours that appeal to you. Decide what makes you interested in them, why they drew your attention, and how they might influence you to take advantage of their services. Good copywriting comes with practice. Write some display ads for your service, and show them to relatives and friends to learn whether they are effective. Encourage these readers to be brutally honest with you—after all, your profitability is at stake. After a time, you will probably become quite good at it.

What if you can't catch on to the art of copywriting? There are two alternatives. First, you can take advantage of the help that advertising space salespeople offer. Many telephone directory salespeople and coupon-mail promoters offer free copywriting and layout assistance as a means of attracting advertisers. Experienced ad-space salespeople know the kind of copy and layout that will pull. Take advantage of such assistance, particularly if it doesn't add anything to your ad cost, *and as long as it works*. Your second alternative is to hire a professional copywriter. Copywriters may not be cheap (charging a minimum of $35 per hour in most markets), but when you consider that their experience can mean the difference between a failed ad and success, it may well be worth the price.

TAXES

We cannot stress enough the importance for any small or large business owner to be in full compliance with local laws, zoning ordinances, and to pay all taxes. There may be a temptation for the small operator, who is also earning a full-time income from a regular job, not to report his or her part-time earnings as part of his or her income. This is a big mistake. If you have registered your company name and have opened a business bank account, the IRS is almost certainly aware—or can easily learn—of your extra income. Don't be foolish. Declare any income you receive from your new business; the penalties you will suffer for not paying your taxes make it just not worth the risk.

Just as you pay income tax on what you may earn from regular employment, you must also acknowledge to the IRS how much you earned from your part-time business. If you are operating as a sole proprietor, this is easily done. The IRS views you and your business as one entity and are therefore taxed as one entity. There are no special taxes to pay because you own and run a business out of your home. On your income tax form, you simply combine your regular gross earnings with your *net* earnings to arrive at your "total income." The only difference is that during the year, much of your income tax has already been withheld at your regular job so that you don't have to come up with a huge amount of money come April 15. You have paid Social Security taxes, federal income taxes, and state and local taxes. But with your part-time business, *none* of your tax has been withheld and you must pay those taxes by the April 15th deadline.

The chances are that the Social Security taxes that you've paid through your regular job will cover your obligation in that department (there is a ceiling of maximum payment). But you will still have to pay federal, state, and local taxes. To lessen the burden come April, the federal government allows you to make quarterly payments during the year on what you estimate you will earn that year. That way, you won't have to pay a large chunk all at once.

If your part-time business is your sole income, making these quarterly payments is a must, as absolutely none of your income tax has been withheld during the year.

When you prepare your tax returns, you—or your accountant—will have to fill out a Schedule C, "Profit (or Loss) from Business or Profession." On this form you will figure your net profit or loss from your business which is added to (or subtracted from, if it's a loss) your regular income.

Deductions

Fortunately, if you are operating your business at home, you are allowed several deductions. If you use a particular room or section of your house exclusively for your home business, the percentages of utilities and rent or house depreciation you pay to maintain it is deductible from your gross sole proprietorship income.

The key phrase that the IRS stresses here is—and they're very particular about it—"exclusive use." If, for example, you use your den as your office during the evenings, but your kids use it as a TV/play room during the day, then in the eyes of the IRS the room is not eligible for those deductions. The room must be used exclusively and regularly for your home business operation.

Other deductions you will be allowed include expenses for:

- Office supplies and equipment
- Subscriptions to professional journals
- Business use of your car or truck
- Utilities (heat and light)
- Repairs and maintenance of the office
- Percentage of rent
- Percentage of home depreciation
- Repairs and service contracts on office equipment
- Insurance for the business
- Business phone expenses
- Business-related travel

There is a limit as to how much you can deduct, however: the amount equal to the total income generated by your business, less the home expenses you could deduct even if you were not operating a home-based business. Mortgage interest, for example, is deductible whether or not you operate a home business, so you must subtract the business percentage of your home from your business's gross income. By doing this, you arrive at the maximum amount for home-related business deductions.

Consult your accountant, a tax specialist, or the IRS itself for more complete information.

Sales Tax

If your state has a sales and use tax, you as a vendor are required to collect this tax on all sales made to customers *within your state*. If your operation is based in New York State, for example, you must collect sales tax for only those sales to customers who reside in New York State. If the sale comes from any other state, you are not required to collect sales tax.

The percentage of tax varies from state to state and, within each state sometimes, from county to county. Again taking New York State as an example, if your business is based in Dutchess County, you need only collect 5¼ percent sales tax; if it is based in New York City, 8¼ percent sales tax must be collected.

It is very simple to collect and pay this sales tax. If you run ads which may pull orders from your own state, or you send mailings to customers or potential customers within your state, then you should include a line like the following on your order form:

"N.Y. State Residents add 5¼% Sales Tax"

To pay the taxes, you obtain the proper forms from your state's Department of Taxation and Finance. How often you must remit these taxes to the state depends on how much sales tax you collect. Most small operations will only have to make annual or quarterly payments, while larger operations are required to make monthly payments (in New York, monthly payments are for total taxable receipts of $300,000 or more).

The forms you must fill out with each payment are quite simple, but you must make payments promptly or you will be subject to a fine of $50 or more.

You will automatically receive the proper sales tax forms if you registered your company, as you should have, with your state as a vendor. When you do this, the state will return to you a stamped Certificate of Authority which must be prominently displayed at your place of business.

Regulations and laws concerning state sales tax vary from state to state, so you should contact your state's Department of Taxation and Finance for complete information.

Part Four:

15 PRODUCT-BASED PART-TIME BUSINESSES

CHRISTMAS CASH

Would you like next Christmas to cost you absolutely nothing? You can make the holiday season the best ever for yourself and your family, and still wake up Christmas morning with cash in your pockets and without bills in the offing. How? By starting a part-time holiday business to help others get ready for December 25.

Christmas is the time of year when almost everyone falls into a spending mood. More money exchanges hands during December than in any other month. People are willing to pay—and pay well—for a happy holiday. And you can take advantage of this trend to make a profit for yourself. Here are five ways to do it:

Marketing Crafts

Carol C. calls herself a crafts broker. She visits every church bazaar, school fair, and flea market she hears about looking for handmade items which are attractive, useful, and well-made. She talks with the artists who created them, asking where else they sell their wares. Carol has discovered that a large number of artistic people are not business-minded, and many market their products haphazardly. She took this information, and built it into a profitable business for herself bringing the crafts to the attention of retail stores in her area.

Boutiques, gift shops, and specialty stores are usually looking for new suppliers. Carol shows samples of products she thinks will sell. When a store decides to stock an item, she asks for a percentage of each sale as her finder's fee. The arrangement works well for everyone concerned. Store managers are eager to add new merchandise to their shelves, the craftsperson's income increases, and Carol earns as much as $200 a week. Christmas is her most profitable time since crafts sell so well as gift items. If marketing crafts appeals to you, consider these tips:

- It is best to have a written agreement signed by the craftsperson, the store manager, and yourself, stating what percentage of the price you will receive for each item sold (Carol asks 5 percent at time of payment).

- Be on the lookout for unusual jewelry. Ask the wearers where they obtained such pieces. Carol found one of her best-selling items this way—a hand-painted, glazed ceramic pendant which she has placed in four gift shops and a department store.

- College bookstores are changing their image. Many of them now sell crafts, and they are often also good places to find talented new craftspeople.

Selling Baked Goods

Diane S., a young mother, has delighted her friends for years by baking gifts for special occasions. One year, three different neighbors asked her to make her special-recipe cookie horns for holiday parties they were planning. Since these were requests from friends, she made the cookies at cost, but the experience showed her that there was a market for her wares.

She let others know that she would be happy to bake holiday orders for them and received orders for several dozen cookies in just a few days. She also took samples to several local merchants with the suggestion that they might want to purchase cookies for customers to enjoy while in their shops. She came home with orders from two beauty parlors, an auto repair dealership, and an optician. Now she is following the marketing methods she used last season and has also contacted several large business offices offering to provide baked refreshments for their Christmas parties.

Diane can spend about twenty-five to thirty hours a week baking, and turns out 100 dozen cookies. For larger orders, she packages the cookies in gift boxes with the lids decorated in gift wrap for a festive look. She charges 25¢ apiece, or $3 a dozen. Since her expenses come to $1.50 a dozen, her profit is $1.50 a dozen or $150 a week.

Tip: Use quality ingredients in any baked item you make and set aside for your own use anything which is overdone or burnt.

Addressing Cards

Maggie A. earned enough cash by addressing Christmas cards to pay for all her gifts and still had money left over. The idea came to her in early December when the annual Christmas card from her insurance agent arrived. Her address had been scribbled, creating a sloppy impression which did not represent the agent well. On an impulse she dropped by to see him and find out who addressed his cards. Some had been done by his secretary, some by his wife, and some by himself. Maggie asked if there might be a need for her to address the envelopes. She told the agent she could do the job for a small fee, and he liked the idea.

She charges 10¢ an address, adding 5¢ if someone wants her to put a signed card into the envelope, seal it, and stamp it. (She always returns the addressed envelopes to the client before mailing them, so it can be verified that the work was done well.) She also charges 5¢ more when a ZIP code has to be located. (For this, Maggie either calls the post office or uses the ZIP code directory at her public library.) She clears about $400 after minimal expenses at Christmas, working about fifteen hours a week for eight weeks.

Wrapping Packages

Theodore F. lives in a retirement village. After his son, a postal worker, related horror stories about improperly wrapped packages which broke open in transit or arrived undeliverable because the addresses had come off, Theodore realized there was a need for package wrappers. He studied the post office's wall posters about how to wrap a package properly, and noted the recommendations for the best types of paper and scaling tape. His next step: a sign in the recreation building of the retirement village offering to prepare wrapped gifts for mailing. He charged $2 per package and cleared close to $200.

Theodore collects boxes of various sizes from liquor and grocery stores. He uses grocery bags, cut and turned inside out, as outer-wrap if the package is small enough to permit this. He will do the wrapping, either at his home or at the customer's, depending on what the customer prefers, since his few supplies are easily transportable by car. In a few cases, he also took the wrapped boxes to the post office for his customers.

Tip: Have the customer write a large address label for the inside of each package. In case the outer wrapping is torn off or the address is blurred by rain or snow, the package will still be deliverable.

Gift Locator

At Christmas, many stores offer certain items at low prices to bring in shoppers on the theory that once they walk in, they'll make all their purchases in the store. Ed S. used this knowledge to his advantage one recent Christmas by keeping tabs on the prices of specific items at each of the major discount and department stores in his community, then advising people where to shop for items on their gift lists. Ed, a college student, built up his business by placing an announcement on the bulletin boards of each department on campus, at his church, and at the YMCA. Word of this service spread quickly. He charges $5 an hour, and estimates that he can help anyone save at least 8 to 10 percent of the total costs of gifts they buy, by directing them to the places with the lowest prices for each item they want.

Ed reads newspaper ads and makes a 3" x 5" card for each advertised item, then spends about an hour a week in each of the major stores, verifying the availability of advertised merchandise, and looking for unadvertised specials which are promoted only within the store. Starting in the second week of December (he recommends starting earlier), Ed had forty-three customers and earned about $300.

Margaret Opsata

CRAFTS HOME PARTIES

Sandy Thomas and Charlene Minor ran a small business selling dried flower arrangements, but they were not getting the profits they expected. They did, however, enjoy making the arrangements and other crafts and country products. When friends repeatedly asked Sandy and Charlene to make their crafts to give as gifts or to decorate their homes, they decided to try to sell their crafts through home parties. Sandy and Charlene now have a thriving home party business called Gram's Country Cupboard, featuring 100 different gift items and fifty items in their Christmas line.

Friends as well as business partners, Sandy and Charlene work as many as ten to twelve hours a day creating items for their business in Charlene's house. "We've grown so much," says Charlene, "that we may soon be moving our workshop out to my barn!"

Before they started selling their wares, Charlene and Sandy attended several other types of home parties to see how they were conducted and what incentives were offered to the hostesses and the customers. After this informal survey, the women felt confident they could offer their own line of quality craft items at very reasonable prices.

Their first home party was at a friend's house, and proved to be quite successful. Charlene says, "At that first party we scheduled three more parties, and we haven't stopped since."

Finding Suppliers

Sandy and Charlene first bought supplies retail, never having bought from a wholesale supplier before. When they did approach some wholesalers, the suppliers would not even talk to them because they didn't have a tax number. So the two women registered their business name and obtained the tax number.

Sandy and Charlene were fortunate that a friend who

owns a small shop not only recommended to them what kinds of gifts sold best, but also let them borrow her business directory of wholesalers. They learned other ways to obtain supplies and names of suppliers: first get the codebar from the back of a package, and then call the Mercantile Library (they called directory assistance for the number in Philadelphia) who will give out the supplier's name and address listed for that code.

In their search for new suppliers, Sandy and Charlene attend local trade shows. Sandy says, "It gives us opportunities to talk to representatives and to see if we can afford their minimum order. We've picked up several good suppliers at these shows, many with 800 numbers to call in our orders." As far as getting wood for their crafts, Sandy and Charlene regularly visit their local lumberyards where they pick up free scrap wood.

Getting Help

The best move for their business was to hire an accountant. Charlene says, "We brought the accountant, Jeff, our notebook with all our receipts. He guided us step-by-step, and referred us to another man who sold us an easy-to-manage bookkeeping system."

Others who work with Sandy and Charlene's business are those who do "piece-work" for them: their demonstrators and the consignors who make crafts and sell them to Sandy and Charlene who then add on their mark-up. Sandy says, "We have not hired an employee because then we would have to supply benefits. We work on percentages, or buy the items directly to avoid getting into that." Whatever item they offer, though, they make sure it is excellent. Charlene says, "We do our own quality-control, because everything we offer (for sale) reflects back on us."

Profitable Parties

The average party brings in $200 to $300, of which the demonstrators receive 25 percent. When Sandy and Charlene first started, they were doing both the parties and making the crafts. Now that they have several demonstrators, the two friends have more time to create their gifts and run their business. They say their demonstrators help fill in the lull periods of the year because they are out looking for more parties to book.

When Sandy and Charlene hire a demonstrator, she is given a "kit" of the items to be displayed at the parties. The demonstrator must purchase that kit (it usually only takes two parties until a demonstrator has earned enough to purchase her kit), and has to book at least five parties. Sandy and Charlene feel their demonstrators take better care of the kit items if they own them.

Besides the 25 percent earned on each party, the demonstrators can get 50 percent off any item they might want to buy. Sandy and Charlene supply them with the order blanks, door prizes, and invitations.

Sandy and Charlene have discovered some other hints that keep customers happy. They do not require the customer to make a deposit on an order, because they feel that limits what people will order. Charlene says, "People will order more things if they can pay later. We get bigger orders, and so far everyone has paid."

With a booking, there is no time limit if someone wants to order something extra, and the hostess will still get her credit. Fundraising helps the business, too, as Sandy and Charlene will give 10 percent toward a hostess' favorite non-profit organization, and a $10 credit for the hostesses when there is a booking expressly for this purpose. One other popular offer that someone recently suggested to Charlene and Sandy was to take $10 off the hostess's bill if she would pick up the order when it was ready. Charlene says, "We have not had to deliver a single order since we made this offer!"

Pricing and Advertising

Sandy and Charlene first added 20 percent to their costs and have since gone to a 50 to 75 percent mark-up. Sandy says, "Even with that price increase, our customers have told us how reasonable our prices are." Reasonable prices, hostess incentives, and good quality have made their business grow faster than they ever expected.

The women have found their best advertising has been through word of mouth. Charlene says, "Classified and display ads did not work for us. Our items sell best when seen. Even though each of our demonstrators carries an album with photos of other decorative items, Sandy and I have found that customers will buy more from the items at the party than those offered in the album."

Sandy and Charlene offer these pertinent tips to other craft makers/sellers:

• Be creative with the crafts by offering a variety at parties, and try to be one step ahead; know what items are most in demand.

- Keep organized. Do not offer more items than can be made. When updating your current line, shop carefully.

- Be flexible. If a customer wants a special order, like something to be made a different color, try to do it. That little extra may pay off in a booking later on.

- Never back out of a party once one is scheduled.

- Learn all you can about merchandising and marketing to keep your business growing.

Priscilla Y. Huff

DIRECT SALES SUCCESS

Every year thousands of men and women across America sign on with a direct selling firm—Tupperware, Amway, or a cosmetic company—hoping to make enough money for new draperies, a new davenport, or some new clothes. They sell a little merchandise to a few relatives and close friends, then they're through. They quit before they give themselves a chance to learn the basics of success in sales. "I am simply not a born salesperson," is a common excuse.

No one is a born salesperson, any more than one is a born doctor or a born lawyer. Sales is a profession. To be successful in any profession one must learn not only the basic techniques, but also how to apply those techniques. Success in sales makes use of all the abilities one is born with, plus all those acquired through education and experience.

What Is Direct Selling

Direct selling is marketing a product directly to the consumer with no middleman involved. Most reliable firms are members of the National Association of Direct Selling Companies. They bring to the public fine products that are modestly priced in order to ensure mass consumption. Most direct selling companies furnish their representatives with a starter kit of essential supplies at below-cost prices. In many instances the investment is under $100.

Sarah Mitchell Gettys was a teacher. In the early 1960s, teachers' salaries ranked among the lowest of all professional salaries. She went into direct sales to earn a better income. She chose a cosmetics line and marketed the cosmetics to small groups of women in the home, providing a service for women who wanted to learn professional make-up techniques and the art of professional color-coordination.

Gettys' teaching background proved beneficial. Her clients were interested and eager to learn. She read books on how to sell to women, and her income grew steadily. Soon she was earning more money than she had ever earned teaching school. She was excited about her new "freedom to earn" and began to share this opportunity with others—recruiting and training a sales organization.

There is an old adage which says, "Give a man a fish and you feed him for a day. Teach a man to fish and you feed him for a lifetime." Gettys taught her trainees how to fish.

Many of them were able to change their lives for the better. They took their families on nice vacations. They purchased a piano or an organ and provided music lessons for their children. They saved money for college educations. They redecorated their homes, bought needed furniture. One highly successful saleslady built a new home.

The rewards of direct selling are many:

1. You can be your own boss.
2. You can set your own hours.
3. You can own your own business with little or no investment.
4. You can pay yourself more than any boss would ever pay you.
5. You can give yourself regular raises as your business grows.

It is only fair to tell you that there are failures, too. There are people who will not work for themselves. When working for a boss, they rise early, are well-groomed, and get to the office on time. However, when they are their own boss, they are still in a bathrobe, drinking one more cup of coffee at 11:00 A.M.

If you can be your own boss and discipline yourself to do what has to be done when it has to be done, direct selling offers a most unusual earning opportunity.

Ten Steps to Success

1. **Be a Goal Setter.** What do you want to accomplish? Do you want to save for college educations for your children? A new car? A new home? You can have whatever you want, but you must want it enough to do the things that have to be done to get it. Whatever your goal,

write it down and set a target date for reaching it. Divide the time period into blocks of achievement that are reachable. Work consistently toward accomplishing each day, each week, each month what you set out to do. Goal-setting is a must in every area of life. Little is ever accomplished without definite goals.

2. **Be a List Maker.** Each evening list all the things you want to get done the following day. That gives you an organized approach to each day. As each task is finished, mark it off your list. It is amazing how much gets done when one works with a "things-to-do" list. Also, have a notebook listing appointments, potential clients, repeat clients, and referrals, and keep it with you at all times. You will be adding to it constantly.

3. **Be Enthusiastic.** Enthusiasm is the high-octane "fuel" that salespeople run on. Enthusiasm generates its own energy. Energy and good health are synonymous with busy, happy people, people who are achieving.

4. **Recognize That the Magic Word in Sales Is "Ask."** In direct sales we don't have to wait for business to come to us. We create our own business by asking for it. Ask for appointments, then you can do business. Ask for business, then you will close sales. Ask for referrals, then you always have a full list of potential clients. Be quietly yet firmly aggressive.

5. **Expect No's.** Realize that no's are not personal.

In sales, as perhaps nowhere else, the law of averages works. Every no gets you closer to a yes. Keep track of your ratio. It will help improve your techniques. Are you getting ten no's to one yes? Is your ratio five to one? Remember, the yesses are your income. Also remember that "no" does not necessarily mean "no." Often a "no" is simply a stall for more time to think. It may be a request for more information about your product or your service. What your client is actually buying is assurance. Assure her by your helpful attitude and your complete honesty, that you want what is best for her. She will most likely respect you and do business with you.

6. **Schedule Time Wisely.** A schedule is the roadmap by which salespeople travel. It takes the frustration out of the day. It assures that the necessary things get done and get done on time. Plan your work then work your plan.

7. **Be Positive in Your Attitude.** Success in sales, as in all areas of life, is 90 percent attitude and 10 percent aptitude. All of us must work at developing habits of constructive thinking. Be proud to be a salesperson. Sales make the wheels of our economy turn. Remember, sales is one of the highest paid of all professions. Statistics show that good salespeople enjoy incomes far above the average.

8. **Have an Office Area.** Most direct salespeople work from their own homes, but it is essential

to have a place where you can work in an organized and efficient manner. An office plus a strict working schedule gives you dignity. Both are absolutely essential for efficient operation and accurate record keeping, so important to the success of any business.

9. **Be Involved.** Most sales organizations offer contests to stimulate production. Include winning contests as part of your business goals. Contests make your business fun as well as adding considerable dollar value to your income. One of my prized possessions is a lovely grandfather clock earned as a contest prize.

10. **Learn to Handle Money Intelligently.** A regular nine-to-five job usually means a paycheck at the end of every second week. Direct sales "reps" (representatives) handle money constantly. Direct sales is instant income and constant income. Therefore, it is absolutely necessary to become an efficient money manager. Money saved regularly and put at interest soon develops a second income in addition to earned income. A long-term goal, which is realistic in direct sales, is to be able to live in retirement off the interest earned on savings.

Would financial security mean a lot to you? If so, ask yourself these questions:

• Am I honest?

• Do I really like people?

• Am I willing to learn?

- Am I willing to work?
- Am I capable of being my own boss?

If your answers are yes, I encourage you to find a good product for the direct sales market, one that you like, one that fills the need of a lot of people, and go to work for yourself! You can turn dreams into reality.

For Further Information

Direct Selling Association, 1776 K St. N.W., Washington, D.C. 20006. Write for their current list of active member companies. Listed are companies offering sales opportunities through party plans and person-to-person selling of such products as cosmetics, toys, household items, jewelry, cookware, skin and hair care, lingerie, health products, crafts, shoes, and more.

Sarah Mitchell Gettys

FIREWOOD DELIVERY

Dale Unger earns extra money by selling firewood. "I started working with my dad who cut firewood full-time when we lived in Idaho," says Dale. "At that time my dad worked at it about three to four days a week." Today, on a part-time basis, Dale cuts and sells firewood year 'round— there is a need for it—and takes home a yearly income that ranges between $10,000 to $12,000.

Even though Dale only works part-time on weekends and holidays, he got hooked because the money makes it worthwhile and the start-up costs are low. Wood cutting is an excellent part-time or full-time business opportunity because you can log in as many hours as you like.

Start-Up Expenses

The woodcutter's most important tool is, of course, the chain saw. Those interested in this field of work might consider having two chain saws, in case one should break. Other vital tools include an axe and a splitting edge (or maul). Chain saw maintenance should be recognized as a likely expense; some practical entrepreneurs, however, have learned to care for and repair their own chain saws, saving themselves quite a bit of money, frustration, and time.

If you make the decision later to cut wood full-time, and your business does well, you may eventually want to purchase a two-ton flatbed truck with a winch. The winch is a must for those with a large wood-cutting fulfillment; winches drag the felled logs, and enable one to load the logs onto the back of the truck to be cut at a future time.

Your total start-up cost can be less than $600. Your initial expenses will include the cost of a chain saw, which can be anywhere from $300 to $500, depending on what size and type of saw you use. Dale suggests a .031 to .051 cubic inch saw because your cutting time will decrease with a bigger and better saw. If you use the saw all day, it can use two to three gallons of fuel. The saw itself holds about one-quarter to one-half gallons. The rest of your tools and supplies will add up to less than $100.

"Before you hop into your truck with all of your new equipment and head to the mountains, you better investigate state laws concerning wood permits," says Dale. Each state has different requirements as to where and when to cut wood. There are regulations on how much wood you can cut, and sometimes there are restrictions on the actual length of cut logs. Check with a Forest Ranger for a regulations booklet. The permit itself will cost about $2 to $4. You'll be required to take a bucket, shovel, and fire extinguisher in case of fire.

Training

Most of your training will come from hands-on education. Receiving guidance from someone already in the business is obviously very valuable, but you should first learn how to operate your equipment correctly and safely. It is a prerequisite of the wood-cutting business to become familiar with the different types of trees and to be able to recognize them. Tamarack, birch, pine, and redwood are just a few of the species with which you should be familiar. Learn which ones are hardwood and which ones produce more heat. For example, pine burns hotter and faster than most other types of wood. This knowledge has other advantages as well: you can ask a higher price for better wood. "In my experience, birch is harder to get, heavier, and brings a better price," says Dale.

Dale always looks for medium-sized trees. Medium-sized trees are more desirable because they are easy to pick up, and haul, and to split, and they measure about twenty to thirty inches at the bottom. They must look clean, however, meaning there is no dirt on the trunk; if they are not clean, they can damage the chain on the chain saw. The ideal trees for cutting are ones that are still standing, ones that have no leaves, and ones that do not have openings at their highest points, thus preventing water from seeping down through the wood.

Since fir is a particularly common species of tree where Dale lives, and is easy to obtain, Dale's costs are lower, and thus he can charge his customers a lower price per cord. The dimensions of a cord of wood are 4 ft. high by 4 ft. wide by 8 ft. long. The price per cord will most likely vary in each state. For instance, one can charge more for a cord of wood in California where cutting regulations are stricter.

The most common log length cut for customers is nineteen to twenty-one inches, because this is the normal length of a wood stove. The amount and size of the wood chopped depends on what the customer requests. "Some people like it cut in four pieces, or in half so it will burn all night," says Dale. "Customers will also specify if they want large pieces or small ones." It is always a good idea to have four or five cords stacked and ready for sale in various lengths so that when you get a phone order you can deliver it immediately.

If you have a truck, a good chain saw and safety equipment, you, like Dale, can be in the firewood business.

Jo Ann M. Unger

FLEA MARKETS

They shopped carefully through wholesalers' and distributors catalogs. They converted sheets of wooden lattice into display panels. They rented a flea market stall, hung their merchandise on the panels, and spread it out on the long table. Now Debbie and Mark Stephenson waited for customers—and looked forward to success.

Flea markets have come a long way since the days when they consisted of low-quality merchandise spread over rough wooden tables set up in vacant lots. That kind of flea market still exists, of course, but today's flea markets may have up to 500 booths in an air-conditioned building, or several hundred booths in specially-designed buildings sprawled over several acres.

Who Are Vendors?

Most vendors are part-timers who work flea markets two or three days a week to supplement their incomes. Others are full-timers who are trying to make a living from their efforts:

- Jim Bickel started selling fishing tackle at flea markets two days a week. He now operates three retail stores.

- Vern and Arlene Wright began selling an automotive metal treatment compound on weekends from an outdoor stall.

- Mildred Bishop began selling sweatshirts and other sportswear from a single booth. Today, she operates from three flea market booths, and wholesales to other vendors.

Today's vendors range from homemakers cleaning out the garage, attic, and basement to the Bickels and Wrights who are serious business people earning a living from their stalls and stores. In between are craftspeople who are selling their own handiwork, retirees keeping busy while they supplement their incomes, and even corporations that find flea markets additional outlets for their goods.

Advantages

Flea markets offer significant advantages to beginners because capital requirements are low and customer traffic—all-important to a retailer—already exists. In addition, since most markets operate only two or three days a week, it is easy to start a business part-time while paying the bills through other employment. Even for a small store, rents can be as high as several hundred dollars a month. In contrast, a stall in an air-conditioned flea market costs about $200 a month, with a month-to-month lease and no additional costs or assessments. The market itself attracts the customers. The vendor will need low-cost signs and displays in the individual booth, but costly outdoor signs and newspaper or shopper advertising are rarely needed.

It may also cost far less to stock a flea market stall than a regular store. That is a good thing since vendors report that outside financing is nearly impossible to find. Most vendors must finance themselves, usually from savings and outside jobs. However, skimping on inventory can be fatal. It's important that the vendor have enough inventory to make it worthwhile for the customer to stop and look.

Become a Success

The vendor, the market, and the merchandise are all important. Vern Wright, who parlayed a two-day-a-week outside stand into a successful bicycle store says, "The people who fail are those who come in for four hours with a hundred dollars' worth of stock and expect to have a thousand dollar day." In flea markets, as in any other business, you have to work for success.

Lois Ploegstra, manager of the Red Barn Flea Market in Bradenton, Florida, says, "The successful vendors operate like a business, with regular hours and good customer service." For example, Ploegstra stands behind her merchandise with refunds or exchanges. Vendors concur that customer service is the key to success.

Successful vendors agree that people go to flea markets looking for bargains. That means merchandise has to be priced below other retail outlets. Look for merchandise in the directories of manufacturers available at the public library, then try the *Yellow Pages* as well as various state and local Chamber of Commerce publications. Other sources can be located through a variety of publications serving the field (see below). Many of these publications are available in the rental office of your nearest flea market.

In some cases, vendors go directly to manufacturers for closeouts, overstock, and irregulars. Making these contacts is often difficult, but worthwhile. Usually, it requires travelling to the manufacturers' plants or offices to meet with them. However, it is not mandatory to stock inexpensive items. Vendors at the Red Barn and other successful flea markets sell merchandise ranging from novelties priced at less than one dollar to high-ticket items such as hot tubs and power boats.

Vendors caution that the merchandise must fit the market. The criterion, vendors say, is the type of customer the market attracts. Ploegstra urges vendors to be flexible in their choice of merchandise. "If one line doesn't provide the sales you want, change to another," says Ploegstra.

Choosing a Flea Market

Some sources say the flea market itself is nearly as important as the vendor and the merchandise. Customers are attracted to flea markets that are clean, convenient, and offer a wide variety of merchandise. If the market doesn't have those traits, the customers won't be there and neither should you!

In some areas, markets may operate on staggered schedules. For example, a vendor can be based in one market for Saturday and Sunday, moved to another on Monday, and still others the rest of the week. One husband-wife team operates booths in two different markets on the weekends, then joins forces in booths during the week. In addition, some vendors operate in the Northern markets during the summer, and move to the Sun Belt during the winter.

Most established markets do little advertising, since word-of-mouth keeps their aisles filled with shoppers. Thus, substantial advertising by a market may be a warning to the potential vendor: the market may be trying to build traffic. That's fine if you can wait for the traffic to be built. However, it is better for you if the traffic is already there.

Shoplifting is a problem for flea marketers as for other vendors. A market with its own security force helps keep pilferage down. Equally important is security when the market is closed (then you don't have to pack up your merchandise and take it home every night).

Market managers are usually helpful to potential vendors; after all, their profit is based on collecting rents from successful merchants. Other vendors can be helpful too, particularly if you aren't going to sell the same kind of merchandise.

Flea markets offer novice entrepreneurs a low-investment entry into retailing. Many vendors have found flea markets to be a profitable source of supplemental income. However, even more people have found flea markets a route to independence.

For More Information

American Flea Market Journal. Quarterly publication. M.H. Sparks, 1911 Avenue D, Brownwood, TX 76801; $10 per year; $3 for a sample.

Closeout Merchandise Moneymaking Manual. E.A. Morgan Publishing, P.O. Box 1375, Huntington, NY 11743; $9.

USA Closeout Directory. Forum Publishing Co., 383 E. Main St., Centerport, NY 11721; $10.29.

The USA Flea Market Directory. Forum Publishing Co., 383 E. Main St., Centerport, NY 11721; $10.29.

Bill Stephenson

INVENTING—MAKE YOUR OWN GAMES

"In 1984 it was just a crazy idea," say game inventors Don Cornelson and Jess Carlson. "Now we're selling games as fast as we can make them." This year their Seattle-based company, Game Concepts, will gross an estimated $750,000 selling three games: Space Estate, Triad, and Four Letter Frenzy.

"There are only a few ideas that will allow you to make big money quick," says Seattle game maker Keith Corner, "and one of them is games. If you happen to come out with one that catches the imagination of the public, it's a way to make money very fast."

One of Corner's friends, fellow Seattle game inventor Rob Angell, is a case in point. "When I met Rob, he was thirty years old and busing tables at the Lake Union Cafe." Then Rob and two friends invented Pictionary®. Sharing Corner's booth at a trade show in Portland, Oregon, Angell and his two partners first introduced their game in June of 1985. Now, according to Corner, all three are millionaires.

Maybe you also have a very hot game idea. But how do you get from here to there—from great idea to actually producing and marketing a successful game?

Research and Creation

First, Keith Corner says, you need to do a thorough search of the marketplace to determine if you have a unique game. The next move is to choose a sensational name and take immediate steps to protect it by securing a trademark. "You don't want to screw up on the name," Don Cornelson says. "It's the basis of your whole product." That means hiring an attorney who specializes in trademarks and copyrights.

While your proposed name is being researched in Washington, D.C., and the trademark is pending, you design a prototype game with everything necessary for people to begin playing it, including an easily understood set of rules. "You should be able to explain your game to anyone in under two minutes," Keith says. "It should be a game that doesn't require too much thought."

Don and Jess spend hours and hours refining the mechanics of their games. "You make up the basic rules, knowing you're going to change them," Don says. "You play the game and see what the problems are. If you have a family game, you can't have it go on for five hours. The object is to make it so within a certain time frame someone is going to lose." In an age when we are increasingly isolated in front of televisions or computers, Keith believes that the most successful games encourage interaction and communication with friends and family members. The best-selling games allow for a large number of players to interact and get to know each other better. And more players can mean more word-of-mouth advertising. If six or eight friends get together for an evening of game playing, chances are that most of them will tell a few people how much fun it was to play, and those friends will decide that they need to buy their own. A two-person strategy game is not a good candidate for becoming an overnight megahit.

Testing the Game

The most important step in the process of creating a game, all three game makers say, is to observe groups of friends playing it. Only actual tests will tell you if the rules are unclear, if it takes too long to play, or if there is too little action to hold players' interest. Keith is adamant about the importance of these trial runs. "You should never go to market without a good thorough testing of the game. You want to test your game with a cross-section of people—professionals, truck drivers, a wide range of ages, etc. You want to find out how people feel about the game, because people make purchases based on their emotional responses."

Packaging is the single most important factor in the emotional decision to buy a game. Keith contends that 60 to 70 percent of the game-buying decisions a person makes are based on how attractive the box is. In addition to a colorful, professionally executed design, he suggests using the package to tell the potential buyer who can play—what ages and the number of players—and whether it's a card game, a matching game, a strategy game, etc. In addition to these basics, you should have some very positive quotes proclaiming that this game is fun to play.

Production

Once you are certain that you have perfected the mechanics of the game and have some idea of how you want it packaged, you are ready to make up a prototype and begin raising capital to produce the game.

Don and Jess raised $75,000 by selling shares in their

business to fifteen friends at $5,000 apiece. "Those people took a big risk with us," Jess says. "And we wouldn't be here now without them." Keith Corner's banker extended a personal line of credit to help him get his game into production.

Keith, Don, and Jess are unanimous on the amount of start-up capital that will be required. Game makers should count on spending between $15,000 and $25,000 to develop and produce their first thousand games. Space Estate, a board game with thirty-five different components including cards, metal playing pieces, and dice, cost more for Don and Jess to make than Keith's card games. Still, Keith says $15,000 would be the absolute minimum for any game.

Once you know that funding is assured and you've found a graphic designer who can translate your prototype into camera-ready art, it's time to obtain bids from printers, boxmakers, playing piece makers, etc. Then you can compute the final per-game cost and arrive at a wholesale price. But you can't just total your expenses and add on a profit. Rather, you need to consider the type of game and how much the buying public will be willing to pay for it.

Jess and Don queried hundreds of game and toy store owners to find out what prices various types of games should sell for. They learned that a game for children should retail for far less than an adult party game. A family game can cost more than a children's game, but still should not be priced as high as an adult game. And a card game cannot sell for as much as a board game.

Once you have your price, your prototype, and a target release date, you're ready to hit the road drumming up sales. "We didn't wait until we had the games to start selling them," Don says. He and Jess obtained a published list of all the toy and game stores in the country. They personally contacted all the managers in the Pacific Northwest. And they mailed colorful, professionally designed announcements and order forms to all the rest.

Don and Jess stress local advertising, in particular radio advertising, press releases, and appearances at trade shows to familiarize the public and the retailers with their games. Shoe leather is Keith's answer on how to market all those games. He tries to personally contact as many shop owners as possible. Some of his largest accounts are with museum gift shops, and he is now expanding into mail order catalogs. His games have been included in several major nationwide catalogs, and he is constantly striving to get into more.

"Getting your game from the garage to the marketplace—that in itself is a success," Keith says. "There are in excess of 3,000 new games produced each year. Less than 1 percent of these ever make it to a second run." Keith does anything he can think of to get his games in front of the people who might buy them. He frequently demonstrates the games for department stores and toy shops and participates in as many trade shows as his finances will allow.

If you think it's possible to skip the step of designing and producing a game and just sell the idea to a big game company, think again. Big companies today do not accept game ideas from inventors. They have their own in-house inventors and game laboratories that come up with ideas. You've got to produce the game yourself and have it sell well for Milton Bradley to come along and make you an offer for a licensing agreement. That's what happened with Trivial Pursuit®, that's what happened with Pente®, and with Pictionary®.

Laurel Holliday

LOCAL COOKBOOK

You can profit from a cookbook that contains the best recipes of the best cooks in your area. Ideally, it will contain about 400 recipes, each one by a local resident, offering what he or she considers his or her best recipe. It will also contain hundreds of little tips and household hints, handyman tips from the husbands of the contributors, items about local stores, and shopping tips by the local merchants on how to save money on daily needs. With such a book you can make up to $10,000 about six times a year, and you do not need a large capital outlay to do it.

Sales of the book are made before you print. The contributors are your major buyers, your equipment costs you very little, and the material for the book costs you nothing. You can create different books in neighboring cities and towns, and have several "best sellers" on the market at the same time.

Begin by choosing a town or city with a population of about 30,000 and obtain a list of all the local residents. The town hall will have a voters' list, or there may be a directory printed for that town or area; the telephone company may print one. Your cookbook is going to contain 200 pages, printed on both sides, so you need 400 contributors. Choose the best areas and keep the addresses you pick (400 of them) several houses apart. The letter you send to each should read as follows (you may change the wording, but we give you this example because we know from experience that it works):

NEIGHBORHOOD COOKBOOK PUBLISHERS
Phone 555-3131

123 Main Street   A.A. Smith
Anytown, Kansas   Editor

Dear Mrs. Jones:

The Neighborhood Cookbook Publishers has chosen this area to publish a cookbook of favorite recipes for the resident homemakers.

We take the liberty of writing you to ask if you will favor us with your favorite recipe.

Since we would like to devote a whole page to your contribution, we would appreciate any tips you may wish to pass along to the less-experienced homemaker, and perhaps your husband could contribute from a man's point of view.

We are going to have 400 contributors to the complete publication, and it will be a valued addition to any homemaker's library.

If we could also be favored with a snapshot, we would appreciate it. Our assistant editor will be calling you within two weeks to see if it is convenient to call on you.

Yours truly
A.A. Smith, Editor

Most housewives will not receive a letter like this in a lifetime, and you will be swamped with phone calls even before you call them. This gives you a chance to tell them you are not necessarily looking for an original recipe, just their favorite one.

Hire three salespersons. Equip each one with notebooks, a sample cookbook as it will look when published, and a good instant-picture camera. This is no cold canvas type of sales work: each call is made on the invitation of the housewife. When the salesperson calls, the housewife will usually have the material ready.

The contributor will want one or more of the books herself, priced to her as a contributor at only $15 each. The actual selling price is not set until after publication, as you are not able to forecast the production cost exactly. She may order as many as she wishes at this low price, with a $5 deposit on each, to be delivered in approximately ninety days. Your buyer is very anxious to receive the finished book with a full page devoted to her contribution, and her name and photo there for all her friends and relations to see. You will find the average purchase is four books. It will take a month for you and your crew to work an area and secure 400 contributors, and gather at least 1,000 orders for books. One test area yielded 1,750 orders.

Now check the *Yellow Pages* of your phone book and visit the dealers of duplicating machines and equipment. The type you need would cost between $4,000 and $5,000 to buy, but the dealer will rent you a beautiful new machine for about $200 per month on a thirty-six-month lease. The machine will copy almost anything, so you can lay out each sheet neatly typewritten with a snapshot in place, and, if possible, a little art work to make each sheet as attractive as possible. Be sure to lease the duplicator of the type that uses any paper, and not the type that uses a roll of paper. Use plain paper of about 20-lb. bond, punched for a vinyl cover with three rings. Print on both sides of 200 sheets. Design an attractive label to fit the vinyl cover. This is an important step to make the finished product attractive, so spend time and money on this step—it will pay big dividends.

In order to print and put these books together, it takes a rather large space. Lay out your printed sheets in piles of 160 each, and put together 100 books at a time. The finished product will reflect the care and thought you put in it, so shop around for an attractive cover (three-ring vinyl). As you need 1,000 copies or more, shop the wholesalers and your cost should be around $1 each, or about 50 percent of retail.

Your books are now ready to deliver, and you have one last harvest to reap. Load your car with sample books and start the promotional campaign. Merchants should order a dozen or more cookbooks at $10 each to retail at $20, and they should gladly pay $50 for a full page of advertising to be inserted in the book. You may be able to collect at least $5,000 in sales and advertising from this effort.

When you finally make your deliveries, you will find many requests for additional books. One test area showed a net profit of more than $13,900 on the sale of 1,000 books. Much depends on the quality of the finished product and the skill of the sales force, but the beauty of this promotion is that once you have successfully promoted a cookbook, you are established. You have very impressive samples to show, and you have experienced salespeople. You will be getting repeat calls for books from each area you work, and the books never go out of date. Keep a reasonable stock of books on hand from each area.

You will notice that the figures given are based on the

sale of 1,000 books. In fact, if the true figures are taken, the net proceeds from a successful promotion, done by a professional sales team with an attractive product, are well up to $20,000. This is indeed a small business that can make it big.

H. K. King

MUSHROOM MAGIC

Wherever the expression "made in the shade" came from, it definitely applies to growing *shiitake* mushrooms for profit. If you have a shady place in your backyard, or can construct a shade cover, you can make substantial money by growing the Japanese forest mushroom on logs. Ray Sohn and his wife Eileen have a spawn laboratory and say it isn't hard; it merely requires patience and an attention to detail. The beauty is that start-up costs are low and the profit potential is good.

The basic procedure is simple: freshly-cut logs are placed in a shady place, inoculated with the spore and kept damp until the mushrooms begin to sprout. One of the pleasant things about the *shiitake* (pronounced "shee-TA-kay") is that the crop will continue to come up until the entire log has been consumed by the fungus, which means about five years of crops from one inoculation. "Usually the peak harvest comes in two years," Sohn says, "with subsequent seasons gradually producing less mushrooms." Inoculate new logs about every two years to have some always at peak performance.

According to a U.S. Department of Agriculture report,

the Japanese *shiitake* industry employs thousands of people and generates over a billion dollars in retail sales, with dried *shiitake* being that country's major agricultural export. The market for *shiitake* in this country is expanding, and offers an outstanding opportunity with these delectable, gourmet mushrooms presently wholesaling at $6 to $8 a pound and retailing at $12.

How to Grow Shiitake Mushrooms

The most crucial part of fungal growth is proper moisture. Once the mushroom gets a start, overly dry or overly wet conditions will usually only retard growth and it will resume when conditions are more favorable. But initially, too high or too low moisture can result in complete loss. During the spawn run, each time the logs are allowed to get dry enough to be dormant it will take that much longer for the logs to fruit.

The best way to ensure the correct degree of moisture is to cut the logs during the winter and store them whole (ideally coating the ends with wax) and under cover to preserve moisture, then cut to length at inoculation time. Small scrub oak makes the best logs, but other woods can be used, too.

Many growers soak their logs before or immediately after inoculating if the logs show signs of dryness. This can be done by placing them in a lake, river, or pond, or they can be hosed or sprinkled. What probably works best, however, is placing the logs in a large stock tank with which the grower retains more control over them.

Light and temperature are the next most important factors in getting a maximum crop. Growth rarely occurs in temperatures under 40 degrees. If you are growing the mushrooms outside, begin the inoculations when daytime temperatures are 45 to 50 degrees if you are working with many logs. Even better results will be had if you wait until the temperature is 70 to 80 degrees, which promotes the fastest growth. "Temperatures over 92 degrees will retard fungal growth, so we recommend a tarp or 'humidity blanket' to allow earlier starts, and to protect during very hot weather," Sohn says. "A blanket will also maintain humidity for the spawn run and during fruiting."

After inoculation, mushrooms grow best in complete darkness to filtered sunlight, but when they are ready to fruit, they do need light. Protect the spawn from direct sunlight. "You'll notice that in nature very little fungal growth occurs on woods in the open, and most is found in the shaded high humidity areas under the canopy of trees. Thinking of that will help you cultivate mushrooms," Sohn says.

Mushrooms are spread in nature by spores. Often, the growth starts in damaged places on a tree where the spore seeds can most easily lodge. The industry now prepares spores under sterile laboratory conditions, initiating growth in wood plugs. The grower only has to drill a diamond pattern of holes in the logs and insert the plugs. Sohn advises inoculating a small amount of logs with a heavy dose of spores rather than a lot of logs with a light amount. "Heavy inoculations reduce competition from other fungi. The really big plus is that the logs fruit sooner because before the mushroom appears, mycelium must completely colonize the log, which heavy inoculations help do," he says.

A good rule is to place the plugs from six to ten inches

apart with about two inches between rows. Inoculating near the wood ends also aids rapid colonization. Once the plugs or dowels of spawn are placed in the holes, seal them with cheese wax, which will protect the inoculation sites from dehydration without any toxic effects to mushrooms or people. For best results, heat the wax to over 250 degrees and paint it on with a brush or turkey baster for the holes; for log ends, dipping is most efficient. Remember to use extreme care since hot wax is dangerous.

One final step remains. Mark each log with an embossable aluminum tag to record the date it was inoculated, the strain used, and the supplier. Leave room to record the fruiting results. In this way, you can keep track of the procedures and products that deliver optimum harvest in your area.

While most of your work is done until harvest time, you can't just inoculate the logs and forget them. In the period of the spawn run (the time it takes for the colonization of the log), it is essential to maintain moisture. During a period of drought or dry winds, the logs made need to be sprinkled or soaked. The angle the logs are stacked at will help retain or lose water, so try to lay them at an angle close to the ground so the water will not run off as freely. A six-inch stripped log makes a good support on which to lay the inoculated logs.

Advertised spawn strains usually promise fruiting in six to twelve months, but it can take longer if the spawn run conditions are less than ideal. Signals that show the spawn run is complete and the logs are ready to fruit is a soft, spongy bark. It's an exciting moment for most growers when they wake up one morning to see the first white buttons forming on the logs.

Equipment

One of the good things about growing *shiitake* mush-rooms is that you can start very modestly and experiment to see if you enjoy the process.

Sohn sells a spawn kit that will inoculate 1,200 pounds of logs for $16.95 (see his address below). The only other equipment needed is a drill, the cheese wax, and a pan to melt it in. Optional, but desirable, are the aluminum tags mentioned, and a humidity blanket. To set up an operation that would promise commercial profits, Sohn estimates that $300 would inoculate a cord of wood (about 4,800 pounds) from which one could expect to harvest 1,500 pounds of mushrooms over a five-year period, if the logs were kept properly. This means a profit of about $2,500 a year on a $300 investment.

Of course, much larger operations are possible. The *shiitake* grown out-of-doors are harvested both in the spring and in the fall, but some growers are putting up sheds to enable them to harvest all year round. Costs are higher with an indoor operation due to the need for heating and cooling systems, but they are offset somewhat by the greater control the grower can exert over the environment.

While the equipment is simple, it is important to take pains in caring for it. Spawn will keep for months if stored in a refrigerator at 34 to 38 degrees, but it must be protected from drying. It's a good idea to put the spawn in a container with a snap-on lid that can be quickly replaced when the spawn is not being used. Close a plastic bag container tightly with a rubber band.

Cleanliness is paramount to avoid the introduction of

competing growths into your logs. Sohn recommends cleaning inoculating tools and areas with a solution of 25 percent household bleach. But remember that bleach is a danger to humans if not used according to directions and should never come in contact with the spawn itself.

Marketing

The United States is Japan's third largest importer of dried *shiitake*. The product is used mostly by Oriental food markets and restaurants. Sohn says smaller growers can easily find a market for their product by simply approaching restaurants. Oriental restaurants are prime targets, as well as produce markets and supermarkets.

"The *shiitake* has a flavor so superior to our common button mushroom, that most supper club restaurants are eager to have it once they have sampled it, because they can put it on their menu as a specialty," Sohn says. Dried *shiitake* exposed to sunlight (or ultraviolet light) converts a compound called ergosterol into vitamin D, and also contains a good source of protein, B vitamins, and minerals, which also make health stores a good target.

Small growers may establish clientele by advertising in restaurant and health magazines rather than approaching the people individually. Larger growers will probably find it more desirable to approach wholesale food distributors. Other growers may be willing to share their marketing ideas with you if you affiliate with a group. The Shiitake Growers Association of Wisconsin accepts members from all states (see address below).

"The demand is there—the mushrooms aren't," Sohn says. It's an open market for someone who has the time and interest. Sohn says he encourages growers who buy his spawn to call him at any time to discuss their problems, and he recommends the book *Shiitake Growers Handbook: The Art and Science of Mushroom Cultivation*, by Przybylowicz and Donoghue, as a detailed guide to all phases of mushroom cultivation.

For Further Information

Cultivation of Shiitake by Gary Leatham, USDA booklet. USDA, 14th and Independence Ave., S.W., Washington, D.C. 20250-2200.

Shiitake Inoculation and Spawn Run Techniques and Indoors Wrap Method by Ray Sohn, 610 S. Main St., Westfield, WI 53964; (608) 296-2456.

Shiitake Growers Association of Wisconsin, 4427 47th Ave., Kenosha, WI 53142. Accepts members from all states. Informative newsletter *The Log* details producing and marketing techniques. Send $12 for membership to: Barb Hermans, Treasurer.

Shiitake News, Rte. 2, Box 156A, Lanesboro, MN 55949. Published by Forest Resource Center. An information clearinghouse for shiitake growers, three issues a year. $25 initial subscription; renewals $15.

Mushroom People, P.O. Box 158F, Iverness, CA 94937.

Mushroom Technology Corp., P.O. Box 2612, Naperville, IL 60565.

Barbara Vroman

PHOTO BUTTONS

When she attended a county fair as a youngster, little did Cindy Adams know that an experience there would eventually lead her into her own business that allows her to make as much as $300 profit for eight hours' work.

Cindy's business is photo buttons, and a photo button she had made as a teenager gave her the idea that gave rise to a successful part-time venture. She works two or three days a week in actual set-up time, and another day or two designing and making unique handcrafted items that showcase her photographs, which are sealed and crimped inside metal badges. The profits are good.

"I set up my booth at a May festival in a rural Kansas town," Cindy explains. "I couldn't believe how many people stood in line waiting. I had to make three trips to a local store for more film supplies. In eight hours I cleared $300."

When Cindy began seeing advertisements for inexpensive badge-making equipment in magazines, she remembered the photo button from her childhood, and wondered if she could make photo buttons of her own to sell at a low price. Cindy contacted some of the companies selling badge assembly supplies (see list below). She found she could purchase a wide variety of products that would enable her to enclose pictures in pin-badges, key chains, belt buckles, magnetic buttons, and mirror buttons. She also found out that other people were already making and selling photo buttons, and had been for years. She started searching for something that would make her photo buttons unique.

"I was already involved in handicrafts, such as tole

painting and sewing," Cindy says. "I decided to put that experience to use in designing wood plaques, cloth rosettes, and pillows that would be a natural showcase for photo buttons. I can also personalize photos by hand-lettering captions for them. Another idea that has increased my business is a folded card with an open circle cut in the front to reveal a photo button inside. People send them instead of greeting cards."

This variety of personalized products enables Cindy to increase sales without adding a lot to her investment costs. "I probably invested $600 in equipment and inventory when I started but I later realized I could have gotten by with less," she says. "In fact, most people could be doing this with less than $200."

Equipment

Cindy lists the following items as necessary basic equipment:

- Button assembly machine
- Button parts
- Camera with instant color film
- Circle cutter for cutting photos
- Simple background
- Small, sturdy work table
- Padded stool
- Display with samples

Other helpful items can be added as the business grows, but are not necessary to get started. These include a camera tripod, a free-standing shelter for setting up at street fairs and festivals, professional-looking signs that attract people to your booth, and several backgrounds so your customers can have a choice. "Many people already have a padded stool and work table," Cindy says. "They might have an instant camera as well. If not, they can purchase one for about $75. It should have automatic focusing and flash, as well as the ability to take close-up pictures. I chose the Polaroid 660 and it has worked out well."

For backgrounds Cindy uses colorful beach towels that she bought for $8 each at a discount store. She simply stretched the towels around sheets of 3/8" plywood cut to 3-ft. by 5-ft., and fastened the towels with large thumb tacks. On the back of each plywood sheet she attached a hinged board that allows the background to stand alone, somewhat like a large easel. Her customers sit on a padded stool in front of the background when posing for a photo button.

Instant color film is the costliest item in Cindy's inventory. Cindy has been buying her film at retail stores at a cost of about 80¢ per shot. Buying film from a wholesale jobber, who wanted a minimum order of $500, reduced the cost to 50¢ per photo.

She sells her photo buttons at a base price of $3 each, so she tries to set up each picture for a one-time shot. "The only time I volunteer to retake a photo is if the subject's eyes are closed in a blink," Cindy says. "Working on location in the street and at fairs the way I do, people don't expect studio-quality pictures. The photo buttons are considered novelty keepsakes and are bought on impulse, so I just get the best shot I can and go with it. I rarely get complaints. I can usually take the photo and have it in the badge and mounted the way the customer wants it in three minutes."

Another initial investment requirement is the purchase of a circle cutter for cutting photos to fit the badge face. A circle cutter can be purchased from most badge manufacturers at a cost of $20 to $50. It is well worth the investment. Probably the largest single investment you will need to make is the purchase of a button machine for crimping the button parts together. These can cost from $30 to $500 depending on the size, durability, and versatility you want. Several companies sell these machines and a list of them is included at the end of this section. Cindy uses a hand-held model because it is easy to pack and easy to use on location. "If I were making novelty buttons in large quantities, I would want an automatic machine for fast production," she notes. "For photo buttons, though, I recommend a smaller, hand-operated model. It keeps your initial investment down, too."

Button parts can be purchased from the manufacturer of your choice, but care should be taken to order the correct size parts for use in the machine you buy. Button parts come in sizes ranging from 1" to 3" in diameter and cost from 5¢ each to 50¢ each. The amount depends on the size of the button, the quantity you purchase, and whether the button is a pin back, key chain, mirror back, etc.

Finally, before you open for business you will need a display board showing samples and prices. This gives you a chance to practice with your camera and button machine so you will have confidence when your first customer says, I want one. "The only practice or experience I had when I started was in making the few samples of my family and friends," Cindy admits. "The more experience you have in taking pictures, the more confident you will be, but I am convinced that anyone can do a good job with the automatic instant cameras that are available today."

Pricing and Location

As for pricing, consideration should be given to marketing costs and economic conditions in the area where you live. Cindy charges $3 as a basic price for a pin-back photo button. She charges $5 for a photo button mounted on a small wooden plaque, and $8 for a ruffled pillow with a photo button pinned to its center. "I think higher prices would certainly be acceptable in many areas, but I want my work to be affordable in the area where I live," Cindy explains. "Satisfied customers have returned to my booth as many as six times in a single hour, having photo buttons made of their children for family and friends. This kind of satisfaction keeps my stand busy and makes me feel good at the same time."

How does Cindy go about finding locations to work? "I try to set up where I know there will be a crowd. To find out about event opportunities I read area and statewide newspapers. Most states have an agency which publishes a list of festivals and arts and crafts shows in their state, too. At each event I attend, I ask others working there where they are planning to go the next week. Many times they will give me tips on events that have been the most successful for them in the past. Usually, a festival or show that has a history of drawing a crowd of people ready to spend money will continue to live up to its name."

Cindy has had limited success with first-time events or small flea markets, although this is not a hard and fast rule.

Some small flea markets are well established and will draw a sizable crowd. You can do well here, Cindy says, if you set up regularly at the same location so people will start looking for you. "For the most part I've found that festivals and community celebrations that attract teenagers and young parents are the most profitable locations for a photo button set-up," she concludes.

Other possibilities include setting up on the parking lot of a busy store, taking photo buttons at school functions, and locating your booth near a local tourist attraction. If possible, you should try to pay a percentage, 10 or 15 percent of your gross income, as a rental fee rather than a fixed rate. Until you know how many customers you can expect on an average day, a high rental fee can be a risky thing.

Tips and Techniques

Working outside in so many different situations, how does Cindy get good pictures when she had no previous experience as a photographer? "My camera does most of the work," she explains. "It uses sound waves and a built-in computer to automatically provide the correct lens setting. It has an electronic flash that blends with sunlight and an automatic variable speed shutter system—anyone can take a good picture with it.

"A little practice will teach you a few tricks that can be helpful. Learn to be patient when looking through the viewfinder, waiting for a shot. Position the subject so they are centered in the viewfinder and nothing distracting is showing around the edges. Converse with them as you work," Cindy advises. "This will help them relax for a more pleasing picture. Watch for hair covering their eyes or dark sunglasses that can make stars with the camera flash. With small children I use a hand puppet to tease them into a smile. Wait for a smile that is natural. A supply of practiced one-liners can help in getting a genuine smile." Some people will have their own photograph they want made into a key chain, pin, or magnetic button. Cindy makes these for $1.25.

Expanding

The business can be expanded in many directions. Cindy uses her ability to paint on wood as an excellent way to showcase photo buttons and increase her profits. Other crafters could adapt their work to photo buttons as well. Some examples might include a family photo button tree, a carved stand, photo buttons embedded in plastic, photo button name plates, a key rack with a photo button of each family member positioned above a hook where his or her keys hang, hand-painted hats that showcase photo buttons, leather bands or fobs designed for photo buttons, and magnetic frames for displaying photo buttons on refrigerators.

"The profit potential is certainly there," Cindy says enthusiastically. "Having your picture on something is a great way to personalize it and there will always be a market for such products."

If you enjoy working with people and want an opportunity to make money by putting your own ideas to work, why not start your own photo button business? Like Cindy Adams, you too could soon be picturing your profits in photo buttons.

Manufacturers of Machines and Parts

Badge-A-Minit, 348 North 30th Road, Box 800, LaSalle, IL 61301-0800.

Badge Parts Incorporated, 2320 West Greenfield Avenue, Milwaukee, WI 53204.

Mr. Button Products, Inc., P.O. Box 68355, Indianapolis, IN 46268-0355.

The Debbeler Company, 3912 W. McKinley Ave., Milwaukee, WI 53208.

Button Designs, Box 34333, Indianapolis, IN 46234; (317) 852-7200.

Roy Halliday

POTPOURRI

The flowers you enjoy in your garden next summer can be a source of income the following winter—right in time for the heavy holiday buying season. Now is the time to plan. Potpourri (pronounced POE-POOR-EE), a fragrant blend of dried flowers, spices and scented oils, is a big seller today with the growing emphasis on nostalgia and romance. Potpourri can easily be made at home from ordinary garden flowers or by taking advantage of free flowers available in every town.

Potpourri is a simple mixture of five basic ingredients: dried flower petals or other natural materials, herbs, spices, essential oils, and fixatives. The resulting fragrance, whether spicy or delicate, woodsy or tangy, depends upon the dried materials used and the aroma of the oils blended into those natural materials.

The basic potpourri recipe can be varied dozens of ways. You make it with a heavy floral fragrance for bedrooms and dresser drawers. You can blend a citrus mixture that will add a tangy scent to kitchens. You can even concoct a mixture with the fresh aroma of a pine forest to add a holiday fragrance to the home during the Christmas season. Rose petals are the primary ingredient in most traditional potpourri recipes. Roses, along with lavender and tuberoses, are the only flowers that retain their natural scent when dried. However, you can use any garden flower to add bulk and color to your potpourri. You can even create a scent with the spices and oils you blend into the flower petals.

Think Color

The best potpourris are enjoyed for their color almost as much as for their scent. Some of the best flowers for color are roses, hollyhock, larkspur, cornflowers, marigolds, heather, purple violets, lilac, strawflowers, blue delphiniums, and lavender. Drying almost always softens the natural color of flower petals (strawflowers are a major exception). Therefore, to get brightly colored potpourri you should choose flowers with the brightest or deepest tones. Most white flowers (except baby's breath) dry to an unattractive beige, so avoid too many of them in your mixtures.

If you don't have a garden from which to choose flowers, now is the time to plan for spring planting. Flower seeds are inexpensive and available from many sources. If you haven't the outdoor space for flower gardening or don't want to get involved with the gardening aspect, you can have all the fresh flowers you need for making pot-pourri free just for the asking. One source is your neighborhood florist. Florists can sell flowers only at the peak of their freshness and beauty. Roses must still be in the bud stage; carnations must be fresh-cut, and perky tulips and jonquils can be no more than one day away from the plant. Now, as hard as they try, even the best florists can't sell every blossom before it begins to wilt. At that point they simply have to discard those very expensive blooms, and most florists are happy to give them to anyone who asks (the only exceptions are those florists who make potpourri to sell as a sideline in their shops).

You will almost be guaranteed of getting all the flowers you need for potpourri if you make a point of visiting florists on Mondays. However, the best times to get literally buckets of free blooms, including dozens upon dozens of roses, are the days after major holidays or events. Valentine's Day, Easter, Mother's Day, and graduation day can be real bonanzas. In any event, be sure to call ahead; otherwise, the flowers will surely hit the trash before you arrive.

Another place to get free flowers is at a funeral home. In most cases, the beautiful flowers used briefly during a memorial service are discarded immediately after the funeral. The funeral directors are usually happy to let you take them.

Regardless of your source, you should begin preparing them for potpourri shortly after they've reached their peak. If you use garden flowers, pick them in the morning of the day they first begin to lose their freshness. Flowers you've cut to enjoy in a vase indoors are fine, too, just use them before they droop. Commercially grown flowers should be dried immediately.

Drying and Preserving

Spread the loose petals in thin layers on trays. You can even add a few leaves to add interesting texture to the mixture; some rose leaves have a fragrance of their own. Place the trays in a dry basement, garage, storage room, attic, covered porch, or any area away from direct sunlight and where the air is dry and still. Allow the petals to dry until they are crisp. Depending upon the type of flowers and the humidity in your area, this step can take from a few days to two or three weeks.

Using this process, you can dry mint leaves, chopped orange and lemon peel, rose geranium leaves, pine needles, or any other natural material that strikes your fancy. You might also dry a few small flowers separately to add a decorative touch to clear glass canisters filled with potpourri. Naturally flat blooms, such as pansies and purple violets, can be placed between sheets of newspaper and weighted during the drying process. You can preserve the shape of flowers with more dimension, such as tiny rose buds or miniature marigolds, by burying them in dry sand. Strawflowers make excellent accents for potpourri. Cut the flowers in full bloom and hang them upside down in a dry, airy closet or garage for a few weeks. The dried flowers are quite stiff and hold their brilliant colors well.

Flowers to be used for accent shouldn't go through the scenting processes described below. You want to retain their delicate shapes, so just put them aside until you're ready to put your potpourri into canisters. Once the loose petals are thoroughly dry, ladle them into a plastic bag or crock with a tight-fitting lid. Any container used for storage at this stage should be airtight. You can continue adding dried flowers to the container throughout the growing season or as you get them from the florist. Just be sure the flowers are thoroughly dry before you put them into the bag or crock. They can mildew or rot if they're the least bit moist at this stage. Keep the container away from bright light and reseal it each time you add more flowers.

Once the growing season is over or you're satisfied you have enough dried petals, you're ready to start the preserving process. In addition to the dried materials, you'll use dried herbs, most of which are available at any grocery store. You can certainly grow your own herbs, too. Some of the most popular herbs for potpourri are: rosemary, tarragon, dill seed, thyme, bay leaves, sage, and marjoram.

You'll use essential oils to enhance the fragrance of the flowers and herbs. These can be found at large health food stores, craft shops, and drug stores. Shop for the best prices. You might want to buy several aromas: rose, lemon, orange, lavender, sandalwood, and eucalyptus. Each will impart its own distinctive "flavor" to potpourri, and will give you a wider variety of fragrances to offer your customers.

Spices are as necessary to potpourri as the flower petals themselves. Most experienced potpourri makers prefer to crush whole spices (cloves, cinnamon, nutmeg, allspice, vanilla bean) rather than use powdered spices. The powdered type can darken the dried petals, obscuring some of the lovely color. Just place the whole spices on a wooden cutting board and crush them with a rolling pin. You can buy these spices at any grocery store.

Finally, add a small amount of fixative to "set" the fragrance of the potpourri and make it last. Orrisroot and coriander are the most common fixatives. You can buy either at grocery stores and health food stores.

Packaging and Marketing

Potpourri is traditionally packaged in two ways for selling. You can pour it loose into large, clear glass canisters, adding a few whole blossoms for the sheer beauty of their color and shape. Potpourri so displayed is often sold at the cosmetic counters of fine department stores. The salesperson simply ladles the potpourri into a plastic bag for the customer. It can be priced by the ounce or bag. If you decide to market your potpourri to stores in this way, you'll probably want to offer at least two different fragrances so customers will have a choice. You might have a floral blend in one canister and a woodsy blend in the other.

The easiest way to sell potpourri at craft and holiday bazaars is in small fabric bags. Select a firmly woven fabric in a color and design that is appropriate to the season. For a summer bazaar you might choose an old-fashioned floral print. For a holiday bazaar you could package your potpourri in bright red and green fabric. In either case, with pinking shears cut circles or squares of fabric about nine inches across. Place about two tablespoonsful of potpourri on the fabric, then bring up the edges and tie with a piece of pretty narrow satin ribbon.

Potpourri can be marketed for a variety of purposes. A small bag will perfume a closet or dresser drawer for months. Bags can be tucked into gift boxes of lingerie, handbags, or sweaters, thereby adding a whole new dimension to the gift.

Jacquelyn Peake

SHOPPING MALL BOOTH

Selling on an occasional basis in shopping malls is an agreeable way of earning an extremely good living. Shopping malls are a powerful marketing area presently being cultivated by a wide range of people with something to sell, from multi-million-dollar corporations, to retired or handicapped people who started out working from a one-room apartment. After all, where else can you find all the essentials for a good income gathered together under one roof: an almost continuous flow of people, personal comfort, and even pleasant background music to provide a congenial atmosphere for the customer. Everything from security to entertainment is thoughtfully and calculatingly provided by the mall in order to promote sales.

With just a little forethought and careful planning, you can take advantage of the most effective form of retail merchandising the world has ever seen—the enclosed shopping mall. Thousands of dollars' worth of marketing know-how are available and you can be part of it.

Promoters to the Rescue

In the old days, shopping malls were simply a string of shops grouped together by developers and planners in an effort to create a shopping area which would comply with off-street parking restrictions. The success of these "strip malls," with their easy parking facilities and tree-lined walkways, encouraged developers to go for bigger and better. Malls grew in size, became closed and protected against the weather, and were anchored by such giants of retailing as Sears Roebuck, J.C. Penney, Nordstroms, and Montgomery Ward who were quick to see the potential in this concentrated form of marketing. However, these big new malls with their glass elevators and flower-filled garden areas, were expensive both to develop and to maintain.

A few very alert promoters began assembling groups of artisans, crafts people, and garden nursery suppliers to offer them as a package to shopping mall management. They proposed a scheme by which they would rent space on the walkways and concourses of the malls, and in these areas erect temporary booths to present a Plant Show, a Crafts Show, or a Home Improvement Show. This arrangement worked well. It provided funds for the mall or the Mall Merchant's Association, and brought increased foot traffic to the area. The promoter, in turn, charged a relatively modest booking fee to each of the vendors in the show. The small-time vendor was now able to sell in a high-consumer traffic location for a fraction of the cost of leasing a permanent store.

Ed West is a show promoter. His shows are all plant, flower, and garden related. "We charge our vendors a fee of $400 for a 10-ft. x 10-ft. booth, and $660 for a 10-ft. x 20-ft. booth," says West. "This is for a ten-day show and includes tables, overhead lattice decoration, and fluorescent lighting." Prices will vary a small amount depending on the mall, according to West.

Kent Headlee's business is called Star Attractions and he has been a promoter of shopping mall shows for several years. His preference is craft shows. Most of the items on display in Star Attractions' shows are handmade. Headlee looks for the smaller businesspeople—the retired person, the home handyman—to participate in his shows. The fee runs between $250 to $400 for a ten-day show, and is usually based on a percentage of sales. Vendors are asked to supply their own tables and displays. Headlee also stresses that city regulations regarding the use of fire retardant material for such things as table covers and decorations are observed by the vendors. And, of course, they must go by the rules and regulations of the malls—no alcohol, no firearms, and so forth. "For several days we are part of the mall, and they expect every one of our vendors to act accordingly," says Headlee.

Contacting a Promoter

It's not very hard to find a promoter. The next time you are in a shopping mall where a show is taking place, ask one of the vendors if they will put you in touch with the person running the show. It's highly probable that the show promoter or show coordinator is in attendance at the mall, often with a booth of his own. Alternatively, go to your nearest shopping mall and speak to the marketing or public relations director. Ask for the names and telephone numbers of a few show promoters.

When you speak with a promoter, ask about fees and booth sizes. Explain the type of product you would like to sell and listen to his advice. The promoter wants you to make as much money as possible as well as to become a regular vendor with his shows. It saves the promoter a few worried nights when he has a team he can rely on. Try to meet with several different promoters and get to know them. Before you know it you'll be moving into a mall one Thursday night just after closing, prepared to set everything up for Friday morning and the next ten days. For you, it could be the start of an exciting and profitable future.

What to Sell

Think as a mall tenant would think when considering the type of merchandise you could successfully market. Avoid products which you can find in every mall: clothing (unless it's really special and unusual), food of any kind, brand-name toys, new books and magazines, photographic equipment, and pets. Mall marketing directors usually request from the promoter of every show, a list of products which will be offered by the vendors. Any product not meeting with their approval is refused entry. They watch very carefully for merchandise which would conflict with that sold by one of the mall's regular stores.

Perhaps you already know the type of merchandise you would like to sell. However, if you have no idea at all, sift through the "items for sale" section in the classifieds of your local newspaper. Watch for surplus buy-outs or new products looking for outlets. Just sit back and consider which type of merchandise you think you could sell. Pick one that appeals to you personally. There's an old maxim that says a salesperson sells best that merchandise which appeals to him or her personally.

Here are a few ideas to get you thinking:

- Tools or equipment which make for easier gardening.
- Swimming pool equipment or gadgets.
- Wood furniture for tiny children.
- Needlework and embroidery decorator items.
- Handmade dolls or toys.
- Collectibles such as stamps, coins, model trains, old movie stills, and baseball cards.

Offering a service is also acceptable in most malls. Here you would offer skills or knowledge gained in a specific field such as burglar alarm installation, kitchen innovation, tree trimming, computer programming, and drinking water purification units. Individual or one-of-a-kind items such as photographs, paintings, sewing, personal hobbies, crafts, and bonsai plants are usually successful. Plants are very popular, especially the unusual, personally grown ones such as miniature African violets, miniature roses, begonias, impatiens, and herbs. Vendors displaying these and similar plants usually have very busy booths.

Establish Yourself as a Vendor

Very few shopping mall vendors would wish to earn a living another way. They like the variety of people, the ever-changing environment, and above all, they are their own boss. Sixty-four-year-old Tom Evergradd sells handmade wind chimes. "I've been selling these for twelve years, and I've seen a few different malls," says Evergradd, "as well as new vendors coming into the business all the time." Evergradd is quick to point out that vendors can have very good days and then very bad days; these highs and lows come with the job.

Lucille Trevor sells tiny cacti plants carefully arranged in small colorful dishes. She is in her early twenties. "I've been selling in the malls for about two years now," says Trevor. "I saw someone selling something similar in a mall in Phoenix, and I thought to myself, I can do that, and so I did."

Shopping malls are a powerful sales tool for the small vendor who has the tremendous advantage of being able to make sales on the spot. The potential customers are there. All the vendor has to do is encourage them to buy. Because the vendor's time on the mall is brief, it is hard to saturate an area with a product, especially if the product is reasonably unique.

Bill Hammond

SILK FLOWERS

Looking for a way to express her creativity in a craft, Honey Formica began to make silk flower arrangements for her home. She loved flowers, and she would experiment with different kinds of flower combinations. Then her younger sister asked Honey to make silk flower headpieces for her wedding, and she wound up making everything from the table arrangements and headpieces to decorating champagne bottles for gifts. Because of this small success, Honey began to think seriously of starting her own silk flower business. If you have an interest in crafts or flower arranging, you might also consider this venture, following Honey's example.

She began by making a list of all the things that she would need to do. First, Honey obtained a business sales tax number from her state of Pennsylvania. Then she had business cards printed with the name of her new enterprise: Silks & Honey. After this, she picked up her phone book and began dialing bridal shops and florists. With the bridal shops, Honey asked if they would display some of her bouquets and arrangements. She also asked if the bridal shop had anyone who made flowers to decorate the shop. She called local florists to get an idea of what to charge.

Honey purchased "how-to" books at several craft stores. "The books were inexpensive and very specific about what I would need to create an arrangement," she says. The local library was also a good source of ideas. Honey gained more valuable experience by working "on-call" at a florist shop. She also enrolled in a non-credit course in flower arranging at a local college which helped her in several ways. Honey says, "It taught me the basic wiring and arranging of silk flowers, the names of flowers, the types of arrangements there are, and what kind of basic tools I would need." Honey has a tool caddy filled with an assortment of pliers, scissors, and wire cutters in her workroom. These she bought as they were needed. Honey recommends that you don't go out and buy tools before you know what you really need. Her total start-up costs amounted to about $300.

Making the Product

On a workbench in her garage, Honey begins her arrangements using sphagnum moss; here she also does any spraying of arrangements. Then she completes her arrangements in her workroom, a converted bedroom. Honey makes many kinds of bouquets: headpieces for weddings and communions; corsages and wristbands for proms; decorative champagne bottles; arrangements for people's homes; all kinds of bouquets and table arrangements for weddings. Honey will make seasonal pieces such as egg baskets for Easter, Christmas wreaths, and for spring she makes her own creations called "Flower People." Honey has even made large artificial trees.

Many of Honey's customers are brides, so she has a

"Bride's Book" with photographs and illustrations of arrangements that she can make.

Finding Supplies

When Honey first began to search for sources for supplies, she found florists were reluctant to give her information. So she spoke to other women who did crafts, and they gave her names of wholesalers who were both reasonable in their prices, and willing to do business with small orders. Once she began to purchase supplies from one dealer, she found that other wholesalers began to send her information. Honey does not hesitate to call new wholesalers for their catalogs and price lists so she can "shop-at-home" for the best prices.

In making up her prices, Honey uses her own technique. She says, "I charge customers the retail cost of the flowers and supplies, plus my time, which varies with each job." The types of flowers used also determine prices. Any exotic silks such as orchids, hand-wrapped, or real silk flowers are the most expensive, while a common polyester flower such as a daisy is less expensive to use. Honey's wedding bouquets may range from a small bridesmaid's at $20, to the bride's bouquet starting at $30, depending on the flowers and the size of the bouquet.

When a prospective customer calls for a price, she tries to listen carefully for what is wanted: a simple, informal type of arrangement or something more formal and complex. She keeps a notebook by her phone that contains pictures of the most ordered pieces with their prices, a sales tax chart, and a calculator with a printer. In a matter of minutes, she can give a cost estimate over the phone.

In the same notebook, with each arrangement is a detailed list of the supplies needed to make the arrangement, such as the place from which the supplies came, and the catalog number. This makes it easy to duplicate the bouquet, and faster to order the supplies.

Advertising

When Honey began her business, she first looked for "free" advertising (and still does). She puts her business cards anywhere they are accepted: grocery stores, pizza shops, bulletin boards of businesses, etc. Besides her business cards, Honey believes "word of mouth" helps to advertise her business. Other low-cost ads can be placed in church bulletins, business newsletters, small ad papers, and any other low-cost publication that might reach potential customers.

Finally, Honey says, "Accomplish as many of your goals in your first year of business that you can. Don't get discouraged, as the first year you may not make much money." But, she says, "you will have lots of fun and gain valuable experience."

Priscilla Y. Huff

TAG SALES

Tag sales are never-ending treasure hunts. For anyone who enjoys snooping into boxes, attics, and garages, has a knack for keeping on top of prices, and has plenty of energy, operating this service can be a sound money-maker, assures Beverly Michael, an eight-year tag sale veteran.

Tag sale clients include retired people who are relocating, anyone moving from one home to another, the newly divorced, families anxious to sell off an estate—even homeowners who have decided to get rid of the old and bring in the new. Many people who want their homes cleaned out are turning the job over to a professional who will examine everything from an elaborate dining room set to old shoes, tag the objects, and assume the burden of moving, showing, and selling.

Beverly, who lists her operation in the phone book as "Complete Liquidation Service," depends on referrals from realtors, attorneys, and former clients. Beverly prefers to be alerted by would-be clients three months before they move. She also expects them to be sure of exactly what they will keep and what will be earmarked for "adult children" who, she has found, can be more sentimentally attached to objects than their parents. She then makes a preliminary visit and conducts an informal inventory. "After I have seen what is at hand," Beverly says, "I urge the owners not to throw anything out. Recently, a client, thinking he was doing me a favor, threw out old magazines and bed linens. Both are good-selling items."

Once the go-ahead for a sale is received, Beverly does a formal inventory, carefully checking the quality of each item. This is when she asks the client to sign a contract. "The owner must understand that I set the prices and I will handle every aspect of the sale, ranging from advertising and arranging the merchandise to removal of the items from the premises," says Beverly. The contract also states that the owner will be responsible for retaining heat and water in the house and will carry liability insurance during the set-up period, the sale days, and when excess merchandise is removed. If any items are removed or sold after the formal inventory or after a pre-sale advertisement has appeared, Beverly is entitled to her percentage (25 percent of the total sale).

Sales are held two or three weeks before a house closing, or the moving date, with a two-week period before, and one week after the sale, also reserved for Beverly's activities. The two preliminary weeks are needed for advertising in local newspapers and for cleaning the furnishings. Prior to one sale, Beverly recalls, "I discovered an antique cabinet in the basement. It was moved to a prominent position where it sold quickly for a lot of money."

Before a sale, sets of items, such as china and glassware, are boxed and shoes are tied together. This is also when every object is price-tagged and when Beverly checks with the town to learn about local ordinances and, if one is necessary, obtains a sale permit.

The action is fast and frenzied on the sale day. "If someone is going to buy," Beverly says, "they will buy on the spot. By the second day, people think objects will go for any offer. But this is seldom so." Two- or three-day sales are limited to "enormous homes."

Attracting Attention

Beverly's duties begin early. She posts signs around town that have arrows pointing to the sale. She attends to last-minute tagging and arranges a desk with an adding machine, sales book receipts, a generous supply of pencils, paper bags and wrapping materials, as well as ropes and tools that expedite the removal of bulky furnishings. The desk is always close to the door that will be used for both entry and exit. Beverly places a large container outside this door filled with numbers for shoppers. By regulating entry by the number, Beverly can maintain a reasonable number of people in the house and keep the sale orderly. She has learned this is an especially important procedure at the opening hour when it is not unusual for hundreds of eager shoppers to appear.

Beverly encourages clients to leave during sale hours. "Their personalities change when they see people tearing apart the home that took them so long to create." She also posts a sign at the entrance that states: "ALL TRANSACTIONS CASH ONLY. OBJECTS IN AS-IS CONDITION ONLY." An interior sign reminds shoppers that merchandise must be removed from the premises by a certain date.

During a sale, Beverly must be alert and ready to sell only at what she considers a fair price. Bargaining is expected, she says, "because this is not new merchandise." In fact, on some items Beverly places bid sheets stating: "If you like this, make us an offer." If the object isn't sold, Beverly calls the highest bidder after the sale. "That's our bit of insurance that the item will be sold," she explains.

When a roomful of furniture is sold, the door to that room is closed. When a better piece of furniture is sold, such as a mahogany desk, it is immediately removed from the major sales area or turned around to deter further interest.

"Theft is always something to guard against," says Beverly. To try to prevent it, she staffs the peak hours of every sale with alert friends and family members. Valuable, small items are kept in stapled bags, showcases, and jewelry cases close to the desk.

According to Beverly's contract, she is responsible for "broom cleaning" the premises. This means that any unsold articles—clothing, pots, pans, furniture—must be cleared away.

The start-up expenditure for Beverly's tag sale service was several hundred dollars. There were printing costs for business cards, brochures, and signs ("WATCH YOUR STEP," "DO NOT ENTER," "ITEM SOLD"). Office supplies were needed—sales receipts, pricing tags, hand tags, and labels. A box of cleaning supplies was also a necessity. "You can't sell furniture unless it looks like new," Beverly comments. She often uses her own washing machine and dryer to give a fresh, clean appearance to linens.

Before every sale, she goes to the house with sandpaper, steel wool, oil, touch-up pencils and crayons, and enamels for chipped furniture. She has also acquired display tables, garment racks, showcases, and matching table covers to help underscore the professional look of a sale. She found them at sales she conducted where she was able to pay minimal prices.

Beverly spends $100 or more for pre-sale ads that run for three to five days in two to four newspapers. The telephone bill and replenishing or renting additional tables and racks also totals approximately $100.

Conducting tag sales can be a full-time, profitable venture, maintains Beverly, "provided you stage at least two sales every weekend through the year." It is important to know antiques very well and the current market value of household items of every type. To keep on top of the market, Beverly is a regular visitor at museums and fine antiques shows where she checks styles, trends, and prices. She is also a frequent visitor at quality re-sale shops and rummage sales, and she garners a wide variety of merchandise catalogs issued by popular retail stores.

It is essential to know "a lot about many different things," Beverly stresses. She remembers a sale when she was offered a dollar for a wrench. "But I knew better. It was a commercial pipe cutter. And it was valued at over $100." She also recalls a punch bowl set the client said she had purchased for $25. Beverly recognized it as a valuable signed piece. It sold for $450.

Beverly says that a tag-sale entrepreneur must be outgoing, be able to think quickly enough to place on-the-spot prices on objects that may not have been tagged, and be able to win the confidence of both clients and potential customers. She also mentions that it is best not to be vain about broken fingernails or cuts and scratches.

Once in the business, make it a policy to conduct thorough inventories, Beverly advises. If there is a workbench in the house, examine every inch of both the bench top and the drawers. It is not unusual to find coins or a rare handmade tool. Sewing baskets, too, can be treasure troves. "Women always threw their thimbles into the baskets and these can be antiques. Pure silk or cotton threads are prized by doll enthusiasts who use them to mend old costumes. Ivory sewing notions, old political pins, and even precious lace can be tucked away into a sewing basket.

"People buy everything," declares Beverly. "I have even found homes for cats and dogs!"

Mildred Jailer

TRASH INTO CASH

If you own a pickup truck, you can cash in on the junk business. Secondhand household goods are either sold for less than its true value, given away to anyone willing to cart it off, or simply dumped for the trash man to pick up. If you know how to resell these items, you can make anywhere from $10,000 to $100,000. You can begin with your own household junk. If you have a garage sale and sell your unwanted merchandise, you will immediately come up with the capital necessary to go into business for yourself.

The Right Kind of Junk

It's important to distinguish between different types of junk—the kind you sell and the kind that has resale value. You'll want to hold onto the valuable discards; they can bring you healthy profits as their value increases.

According to Don Petersen of Westlake Discount Furniture, you will find that just about anything in your home is worth keeping, providing that the item is in decent shape, shows little wear, and has no broken pieces. Petersen started his business out of his home ten years ago. Today, he has over 6,000 feet of showroom space, owns three buildings, five houses, and is constantly pursuing potential sellers and buyers with good deals on used furniture. But furniture is not all that Petersen has to offer at his store. Customers can purchase tools, woodworking equipment, fishing gear, used office furniture, watches, clocks, radios, CBs, TVs, fitness equipment, rugs, beds, and musical instruments. One person's junk is truly another person's treasure.

Getting Started

You could begin your business venture by cleaning attics, cellars, or garages for junk, and charge for gas and disposal site fees. You could also start the same kind of business on the premise that the goods worth purchasing are bought first and taken away. Whatever is left will be carted to the dump with the cleaning service included. You'll want to purchase the valuable merchandise and get it out of the way before offering to clean up the attic, cellar, or garage. The merchandise that you carry off is yours to keep whether or not it is worth anything.

Once you establish yourself in this business, your next step is to offer your services to potential customers. Advertising need not cost you much. You can place ads for free in your place of employment, laundromats, supermarkets, hardware stores, at homes where garage sales are being conducted, flea markets, and hair dressing salons. Your ads should be done on 3" x 5" index cards, preferably ones that are colorful. Make sure you include information on pricing; this will eliminate a barrage of phone calls from people who are "just shopping around." Homemade posters are also a good way to advertise. Include before-and-after pictures of a clean-up job. If this doesn't appeal to you, try inserting fliers in mailboxes and at real estate offices. Going directly to the source (someone is moving and needs to have unwanted items carted off) could prove to be your most successful step.

Evaluating Your Merchandise

One way of making sure you don't pay too much for merchandise is by doing comparison shopping. Go to used furniture and household goods stores in your area. You should also try giftware shops, antique emporiums, and bookstores. By doing this, you will see what retailers are asking for their merchandise. Remember that this price is based upon what the shopkeeper thinks he or she will get for each item, and not what the retailer actually paid for the merchandise.

The junk business is one of the easiest small-business ventures you can get into. With luck and perseverance, you should be making a profit in no time at all.

R.T. Edwards

WOODEN TOYS

Since 1965, Bob Zarse has been a full-time farmer. His love for farming led him to become an active collector of farm toys. However, this part-time hobby grew into something else, something unexpected—a successful and thriving farm toy mail order business. Zarse's Farm Toys is a family-operated home business which has grown remarkably since it started less than ten years ago by Bob, his wife Kathy, and their sons Randy and Chuck.

Their biggest selling items are toy tractors and toy trucks. Children and collectors can buy the inexpensive 1/64 scale tractors, the bigger and more expensive 1/16 scale tractors, pedal tractors, and books which Bob has written alone or co-authored. Bob also designs exclusive custom imprint 1/64 scale trucks and gravity wagons for interested customers. Only two other businesses in the U.S. do a comparable mail order farm toy trade.

The Zarses started business in their basement, then moved out to the garage. A warehouse has been built on their property to accommodate their growing toy inventory. Farming is still the most important part of the Zarses' lives, but their mail order business continues to take more time and effort.

Bob's interest in toy tractors began when he started purchasing a toy tractor for each real tractor he owned. Then he began to sell them, and gradually the business grew. "When I started the mail order business, I was the only one doing the work," Bob says. "I would come in from the field at night and pack orders. Farming and the mail order business go well together because our slow time in mail order is during planting and harvesting—that's when I am busiest farming. The toy business picks up in the summer and winter, and that's when I've got the most time."

Bob's business is thriving, and over 40,000 orders have been shipped throughout the world including all fifty states, provinces of Canada, West Germany, Italy, England, Australia, and parts of Africa.

Being a collector, a farmer, an author, and a farm toy dealer gives Bob an advantage in this unique business. He understands his business from every possible angle. For example, the farm toy collector who collects every International Harvester tractor ever made is looking for a complete and accurate collection. Bob can supply the collector with accurate and up-to-date information on farming and farm toy collecting.

Farm toy collecting is one way for the avid collector to stay in touch with his or her farm heritage. "Farm toy collectors usually have a tie to the farm," Bob says. "Some of them may be two generations away from the farm. In essence, they are collecting part of their family's history."

Bob and co-author Eldon Trumm write guides for the farm toy collector. The books sell well—this spring a new book, *Trumm and Zarse's: A Guide to Collecting Toys* (Case and Poclain Toys Volume 1) will be released and sold through mail order brochures and advertisements. "We built our mail order business on service," Bob says, explaining his success. "On the same day the order comes in, the order is shipped out. I believe we keep ahead of our competition because of service. We keep our customers because of service."

Zarse's Farm Toys—started as a part-time hobby—is now one of the largest farm toy mail order businesses in the U.S. This unique family-run business provides a good income for this farm family. Luckily for Bob Zarse, his business continues to grow and prosper.

Ingrid Moe Miller

Part Five:

14 SERVICE-BASED PART-TIME BUSINESSES

CALLIGRAPHY

Calligraphy, the art of beautiful writing, can also be a way to write yourself a spare-time income. It's an ideal way for anyone with no formal art experience, training, or talent to make extra money at home. Beginners at this easy-to-learn craft can start making money by addressing envelopes, filling in certificates, and making place cards for formal dinners. With some experience, you can create publicity flyers for schools and churches, design invitations and birth announcements, and letter signs for businesses.

The first thing you have to do is learn to do calligraphy. Learning the basics is easier than you might think; check with your local community college, park districts, museum, or church. If you can't find a class in your area, there are several fine books available (see below). The important thing is to practice. Even the best teacher in the world can't give you the polished, consistent look practice provides.

Beginning

To begin you need to purchase a calligraphy pen. If you take a class, the instructor will recommend a brand and size. If you're learning from a book, chances are the author will specify a pen. Most students start out with a standard calligraphy marker available at art supply, stationery, and office supply stores, or by mail order. The least expensive choice is a marker which has a limited lifetime (unlike pens which can be refilled); its point tends to lose the necessary sharpness after awhile, but for the investment of about $1, a marker lets you "play around" with calligraphy and see if you'd really like to perfect this craft. Slightly more expensive, but still available for under $10, are No Nonsense Calligraphy™ pens made by Shaeffer. These pens come with three different nibs (points), ranging from broad to fine, and use standard Shaeffer ink cartridges.

The only other things you need are good quality paper, a sturdy writing surface, and time to practice. Read the book you've chosen, practice one alphabet until you master it, and *use* your calligraphy. There's no comparison between writing endless rows of letters and actually addressing an envelope with your new skill. As soon as you've learned one alphabet, start practicing a second. Most clients need one of three standard types: italic, uncial, and black letter (similar to Old English).

Freelance Calligraphy

As a freelancer, the first things you'll need are business cards. Have them printed with a twist, however, and provide the printer with camera-ready copy that you do yourself—in calligraphy, of course. Talk to your printer about how to do this. A calligraphed business card is different and provides your potential clients with an immediate sample of your work. Be sure to keep the amount of information on the card simple: your name, telephone number, and calligraphy should be enough.

You'll also need to advertise. A local shoppers' paper, which offers low rates for a display ad, is a good place to begin. You can also design a small flyer in calligraphy and leave copies of it on bulletin boards and at supermarkets. The calligraphy alone is an attention-getter. Printers are also approached by people who need calligraphy, so be sure to leave some business cards with your printer.

Getting Work

Who is your potential client? Anyone sending out wedding invitations will consider paying a calligrapher to address the envelopes and fill in the placecards for the dinner. You address the envelopes from a list of the guests (request that it be printed or typed), and then return them to the client for stuffing and sealing. Rates for this vary, but you could get $1 per envelope on average, with an extra 25¢ per place card. With some experience, you should be able to address eight to twelve envelopes an hour.

Businesses also need freelance calligraphers to letter signs, prepare camera-ready copy for flyers, or even design special greeting cards. Schools and organizations will contact you to fill in or even create award certificates. The fees for these kinds of tasks are harder to gauge, but you can set your goal for a certain amount per hour and charge with that rate in mind.

You can also contact wedding consultants and party planners to try to reach a wider audience. They usually charge a commission, but the exposure may be worth it.

If you don't mind sitting at art fairs, this is a good way to exhibit your calligraphy. It takes a big investment: you'll have to pay an entry fee, create a display, mat and frame your work, and perhaps pay a percentage of your sales to the promoter. However, there are advantages to the art fair circuit in terms of increased exposure and future commissions.

Doing the Job

The next step, after establishing yourself as a professional calligrapher and attracting interested customers, is dealing with prospective clients. Let's say someone contacts you about possibly addressing her wedding invitations. You agree to meet with her and show samples of your work. It's a good idea to have a prepared portfolio of your work to show clients.

Once the client settles on a style of lettering, discuss ink color. Black is standard, but ink is available in many different colors. If you use a cartridge pen, you'll need to know which colors are available for your particular pen. Insist on legible copy to work from, especially if you're addressing envelopes. Don't agree to look up ZIP codes or check your clients' spelling—that's their job (unless they want to pay you to do it). Remember, the more accurate the copy, the easier and better your job will be. Be sure you know how names should be prefaced (Mr., Mrs., Miss, Ms., or Master) and how the client wants names of states to be written—the full spelling or the post office's preferred two-letter abbreviation. Finally, agree on a price and a delivery date.

Go home with the envelopes, your pen, and ink—and write! If you pre-line each piece in pencil, be sure to let the ink dry before erasing. Work carefully and in private, pay close attention to your copy, and check often for errors. Break when you're tired and don't eat or drink while working (one drop of coffee can ruin an otherwise perfect piece). Have someone else check your work for accuracy after you finish.

When you deliver the calligraphy, be sure to include a

business card or two along with the bill. Word of mouth is a powerful advertising tool for calligraphers.

For More Information

Calligraphy for Fun & Profit by Anne Leptich & Jacque Evans ($9); *Advanced Calligraphy* by Katherine Jeffares ($9); *Calligraphy—The Art of Beautiful Writing* by Katherine Jeffares ($9). Each title available from E.A. Morgan Publishing Co., P.O. Box 1375, Huntington, NY 11743.

Supplies:

Dick Blick Central, P.O. Box 1267, Golesburg, IL 61401. Dick Blick carries pens, paper, books, and other supplies for calligraphers and artists.

Dover Publications, Inc., 31 E. Second St., Mineola, NY 11501. They have several catalogs of books on fine art and crafts.

Deborah Stern Harris

COURT TRANSCRIBER

Marsha Chandler ran a typing service out of her home which brought in a sizable part-time income for her family. Then one night she received a call from a court reporter who asked if she'd type depositions and court transcripts as an adjunct to her typing business. Of course, she said yes. But soon there was so much court work that Chandler could scarcely find time for the rest of her clients. Eventually, she decided to specialize in just court transcripts. Ten years later, she still works at home, still produces court transcripts, and most important, still makes a good living in her own business. But the look of the job has changed. The court-reporting industry is now using computers extensively.

Scoping for a Living

The term "scoping" is an industry term that means the editing of text on a computer screen. Many court reporters still transcribe court proceedings on the same old machines you've seen on a dozen police shows and courtroom dramas, but now the machines are equipped with computer memories which may be dumped after each job into a translation unit. The translation unit converts the court reporter's notes from shorthand into English. However, even the best reporter does not get a 100 percent translation and proper names and punctuation usually must be added. At this point, the scopist takes over to "clean-up" the transcript.

As more and more court reporters across the country begin to use computerized transcripts, the need for scopists will only increase. Presently, there is no school where you can train to become a scopist. The best method for training in the field at the moment is to contact a court reporter who is willing to train you to be his personal scopist (and there are many such reporters). You can contact local court reporters by calling your county courthouse and asking for the court reporters' offices or by looking in the *Yellow Pages* under "Reporters, Court and Convention." If you call the county, you will be calling court reporters who work in court; if you call court reporters listed in the *Yellow Pages,* you will be calling private deposition and convention agencies. These court reporters handle different types of work, but they are all converting to computers and will probably have a need for new and talented scopists.

Your chances of succeeding in this field are greater if you can type well, if you are a good speller, and if you have a good grasp of word sense and punctuation. Without these skills, text editing will be difficult. But with these basic skills, text editing can be a very comfortable source of income for a home-based business. Chandler found it to be very flexible as well. Although she works under court deadlines, she works her own hours and calls her own shots. And if a court reporter lives too far away for a pickup to be practical, computer disks containing the job can be mailed back and forth via UPS at very little expense.

Computers in the court-reporting industry are not much different than anywhere else in the business world. There are a handful of competing major manufacturers of these specialized computers for the court-reporting industry. It makes sense to buy the computer that would be most compatible with the largest number of court reporters. Chandler uses an Xscribe, but the other machines in the industry are also very good; don't make a decision on machinery until you know which company has the highest sales volume in your area.

Scoping Opportunities

Many court-reporting firms hire proofreaders as well. If they like your proofreading abilities, they may train you as a scopist somewhere down the line. Chandler has done just about everything which is remotely related to court reporting, with the exception of court reporting itself. Over the years she has managed a reporting firm, transcribed, scoped, proofread, done the billing, done the binding, answered the phones, and trained new reporters.

Scoping requires a good deal of skill, training, and know-how, but that shouldn't turn you off—the field is still wide open. There are very few people who have training and background in scoping. At one time there were many skilled transcribers, but few of them made the transition to computerized output. The reasons were varied and ranged from the need to be able to read court reporters' notes, to the commitment of purchasing a computer.

Working in the court-reporting support sector has proven challenging and rewarding. And now more than ever there is a shortage of skilled individuals and a need for you. If you like computers, work well with the written word, like a challenge and want to work at home without giving up a good income, scoping is a field that is waiting to be discovered.

Marsha Chandler

DEFENSIVE DRIVING INSTRUCTOR

If you like talking before groups, being a part-time, self-employed defensive driving instructor may be the field for you. It is relatively easy to learn because you will be teaching people who already know how to drive, and the class material doesn't change much as time passes. And there is little competition. You won't have to meet people to sell the idea to them since they will be coming to you.

Requirements

You will need a special license. Contact an insurance broker or your state trooper headquarters. Or try the Department of Public Safety or the Department of Motor Vehicles. They can tell you how to become certified.

You will give classes to people who want to learn safe driving methods, who have been ordered to the classes by a judge for driving while intoxicated, or who just want to lower their insurance rates. The classes may last as long as eight hours, and can be conducted on a Saturday or in two four-hour evening sessions during the week. Since many people who take these classes work during the day, they will want their classes to be after hours. These hours may also benefit you if you have another job.

Equipment and Supplies

To supplement your talk you will probably need a television and VCR on which to play several safe-driving video tapes. Your state may require you to follow a specific book outline, in which case you may have to supply textbooks as well.

You can conduct classes at work sites or in community rooms of banks or churches. Some classes are even held in banquet rooms of restaurants. A local business or public building may let you use their conference room. In many cases, they won't charge you a fee because your class is a public service. You must, of course, reserve the meeting places and make sure there will be enough seating for your students. Your class size could vary from ten students in small towns to fifty in cities, but you will want to determine your optimum class size and aim for that. When there are too many students, they may find it hard to see the video unless you have several televisions stationed around the room.

You will probably need to drive to the place where the class is held. If you live in a large city, you may want to hold the classes in a different part of the city each time, or you may be successful always having the class in the same place. In small towns, you will find it more appropriate to hop from community to community to be near the students, eventually making your rounds back to the first town to start all over.

Advertising

Make flyers listing your phone number and the class dates, times, and places. These can be typed or done with press-on letters (available at an office or art supply store), or you can use computer software designed to make such flyers. Ask businesses, especially those with lots of foot traffic, to let you put up the flyers. Run a classified ad in the newspaper about two weeks prior to the class. If you have a daily newspaper, you may want to run the ad more often. For continuously held classes in one area, run a display ad and schedule the students for specific classes as they call in. The display ad could have a cut-out box for the students to fill in and mail to you. Classifieds are cheaper, but displays can work better.

Because this business is a public service, you may find the newspaper editor happy to run a short item about the class for free. Write up a couple of paragraphs and inquire. Even a radio station may do this. It doesn't hurt to ask. Once you are in business, you will know your local media and what they will do, having regular contacts before each of your classes. Publicity is a good complement to advertising. Make your presence known to justices of the peace and municipal judges. They may refer (or even order) persons guilty of drunken driving to your classes.

Cost

Figure a cost which will cover your meeting room fee (if any) and your travel cost, depending on the estimated number of students. Your Department of Public Safety office or your local courthouse may know the going rate for such classes in your area. If it is too expensive, people who are merely trying to save insurance costs will shy away. Feel this out in your community to see what's best.

The initial cost to you is the certification fee and whatever classes are involved to learn how to teach defensive driving (somewhere around $300 in cost), as well as the purchase of the TV and VCR; one option is to rent them. Each class would have the additional cost of the room rental cost, travel, and your time. If books are required, you may have to purchase them.

Some people make careers of teaching this class. Others just do it as a permanent sideline. While it is a rewarding and certainly a needed service, one instructor comments that he is glad he does it part-time because it gets tiring giving the same class repeatedly eight hours a day. He needs a break of a few days each week. Nevertheless, this is an often overlooked specialty where you won't have much competition.

Sandra G. Holland

DELIVERY SERVICES

Several specialized delivery services have sprung up over the last few years aimed at one of the strongest buying segments in America: the college student. Recent studies show that the average college student has over $4,000 in disposable income (above and beyond tuition, fees, books, and basic room and board) per year. Add another rather well-off buying segment, university employees, and the college market becomes a boon to anyone with good entrepreneurial skills. Here are some delivery businesses you can start that capitalize on this market.

Survival Kits

One of the first major delivery ventures to target the college market was the so-called "survival" or "final exam kits." These kits are now available from several small firms at many of the larger campuses, but most smaller campuses and junior colleges are untapped. The kits usually contain food, flowers, soda, candy, a trendy toy or two, and a humorous card. Actually, you will not sell the kits to the students directly, but to their parents. The parents then send the kits to their sons and daughters during finals week, on their birthdays, or on other special occasions.

The best way to market the kits is to obtain a student directory that lists the students' home address. Most college directories now list that information. Send a direct mailer, consisting of a color brochure with a picture of two or three kit choices, to the parents. Pricing of the kits is rather simple: pre-price your goods and delivery costs and add in the margin for profit.

College delivery services have continued to grow and change over time, and you can often expand the innovation found on the college campuses to the general public. Or, conversely, you can modify general services to attract the college market. The college "survival kit" has its public counterpart in food and floral deliveries common on Valentine's Day and Easter.

Party Service

The success of the survival kits spurred other entrepreneurs to attempt a variety of unique delivery services to students. One example is a party service. After all, what would college life be without parties? With such a service available, all the would-be party holder has to do is call the service and all of the necessities of the party are delivered for one price. It saves the party holder time and, in some cases, even money.

One instant party firm is Party Helpers based in Los Angeles. The company was started by college students at UCLA and began by working with student parties. Peter Siegel, the company owner, saw the opportunity for a party delivery firm by attending several parties around campus which he noticed were poorly planned. Siegel began the company with the help of several other college students as a way of making a little extra money.

Party Helpers started slowly, working a few small parties around campus until the firm's reputation grew. To spread the word about his service, Siegel made sure that all party-goers knew he catered the party. Siegel's on-campus business grew. Eventually, Party Helpers' reputation stretched beyond campus boundaries throughout the Southern California area. They soon developed such a reputation for delivering complete parties that they began to host private parties for people outside the university—over 1,000 parties a year.

Food Delivery

Boston University graduate Peter Stein exploited an opportunity in Boston that had previously been ignored. Some food establishments did deliver their own food, but there was no central food delivery service for a variety of foods. "No one could order a pizza and a little Chinese food before us," says Stein. "Better than any one restaurant could, we are able to serve groups that have widely varying food tastes."

Gourmet Grub delivers foods ranging from ice cream to Thai cuisine. Nine food establishments have contracts with Stein allowing him to deliver their food. "I check out every restaurant before I sign a contract with them to assure me of their quality," Stein says.

The contracts are the crucial step in the business formation, according to Stein. The restaurants must agree to let you deliver their food, exclusively if possible, and let you have their food at a reduced price. "Most of our profit is in the difference between the menu price and the price at which the restaurant will sell it to us," says Stein. "We add on a small amount to the menu price also, but that is a very small price boost."

Laundry Pick-Up and Delivery

College delivery services run in Stein's family. His brother Michael has a laundry delivery service. Michael, a student at Skidmore College, is the owner of Tucker's Laundry, a pick-up and delivery laundry service. "I really inherited the company and the idea," says Michael Stein. "A senior and fellow tennis team member came up with the idea. Within a year after he graduated, I bought the company."

Under Stein, the company has seen impressive expansion. Each year since he started running Tucker's Laundry, the company has shown a 40 percent growth rate. "Our business plan is simple," says Stein. "We have a drop box right on campus where students can deposit their dirty clothes. We guarantee to have the clothes delivered to the student's room within a day." Stein also employs three students to pick up laundry at the residences. Tucker's has done so well within the student community that the business is now serving university staff and customers off campus. Tucker's Laundry picks up, washes, and delivers about 700 pounds of laundry a day.

The key to the firm's rapid growth, according to Stein, is the care they take with the clothes. "Trust and reputation are the most important thing about this business. People are very particular about their clothes," Stein explains. To assure quality and careful washings, Stein has contracted with several local housewives whom he has thoroughly tested. The core crew that does the washing has a profit-sharing option, as do the delivery people; this gives them the incentive to do quality work.

Grocery Delivery

Some delivery services fill niches that larger concerns once commonly filled. That is the case with the grocery delivery business. What individual grocery stores once did, entrepreneurs are now doing—home delivery. Connie Long, a student at Wichita State, the home of the Association of Collegiate Entrepreneurs, owns and operates a grocery delivery service called Grocery Express.

The grocery delivery service is a fairly easy one to operate. Long has accounts at three of the larger supermarkets in Wichita to assure that she gets the best prices for her clients. She takes the orders by phone, buys the goods, and then delivers them to the customer's door. "The major market is two-earner families. Most of them are employees of the university. University employees are very busy and need this kind of help," Long says.

Grocery Express depends on promotion to get new clients. Long has appeared on local TV and has been featured in several local publications. She also circulates flyers at grocery stores.

The college delivery service market is as diverse as the college scene. A smart entrepreneur living near a college or university campus can exploit the lack of transportation and free time common in that market. Wise campus marketers say that if there is a regular use for an item, then a delivery service for that item is possible and profitable.

William and Wendy Ball

FREE SCHOOLS BRING HIGH PROFITS

If you have an interesting skill, such as painting, computer programming, photography, or dance, you could teach it at an "Open University" and make money. Or you could start your own school and let others teach.

"Tantra," reads the ad in Boulder Teachers' Catalogue, "is the art and science of using desire, passion, and sexuality as vehicles to expand consciousness and attain liberation." Max West and Cindy Eaton will teach "ways to generate, circulate, and focus large amounts of sexual energy . . ." for $45 a head. Interested? So are lots of other people.

Courses are open to the public and last a few hours or a few days. Students enroll by phone or mail and pay from $15 to $85 by check or credit card. Catalogs advertising the courses are distributed at supermarkets, restaurants, and other public locations. Let's take a look at what it takes both to teach a course, and run a free-school catalog.

Teaching

You don't have to be a college grad to teach. Most people have skills and experiences others find interesting. Singing instructor Cara McMillan says, "Adults have very different reasons for taking courses than children do. They want information, they want to get out of the house, and they want a reality shift away from work. They often want physical exercise, and a social life with other people who are interested in the same things, and a safe environment. The more of these needs you meet, the more students will come back."

The Advertisement. The catalog ad is the key to getting students. An ad with zing, which offers solutions to problems, needs or desires, and has broad appeal will attract many customers. Teachers generally write their own ad, which is reviewed by the catalog publisher before printing.

- *Offer solutions.* "Have more fun taking better pictures by learning how your 35mm camera works . . . ." A shopping list of topics can attract students who need to know a few specific things, as well as novices who need to learn it all.

- *Appeal to as many people as possible; write for an emotional response.* "Would *you* prefer to be a human *being* or a human *doing*? This workshop is an opportunity to feel more loving with yourself while experiencing intimacy in daily life. Contact, breath work, movement, and other guided experiences will enhance this workshop." Here "you" appeals to everyone regardless of age or sex, and "loving" and "intimacy" elicit a positive emotional response. "Contact" and "workshop" add zing by implying students will actually be intimate in class.

- *Connect with people's real world.* "Work with your individual powerful solutions." Emphasize real results the student can put to work.

- *Highlight important points with italics, upper case letters, or underline.* "Each student will write a one-page *synopsis*, a *treatment*, and a 125-page *screenplay*." These emphasized items will stand out in students' minds, even after reading a dozen other course ads.

- *Schedule courses on evenings or weekends,* since most people have jobs or classes weekdays. Some teachers offer several sections on different days.

- *Give credentials.* "Sylvia has been training and showing dogs for twenty years. She has been an animal handler for television shows and commercials." Your biography should inform students why they can trust you.
- *Quote enthusiastic students.* "I really got my money's worth from this course!" Play it straight and make sure that quotes are authentic and represent students' true feelings. Phonies are bad news to catalogs and other teachers since they damage good reputations and turn away repeat enrollees.

Enrollment. Some free-school catalogs are simply an advertising medium and leave all enrollment and fee details to each teacher. Others collect payment by mail or phone from students and pay the teacher after the course has run.

Editor Duane Fry offers advice to new teachers. "Boulder Teachers' Catalogue publishes and distributes the catalog containing your course description. We do not do the registration or collect tuition. Your phone number is in the heading of your course; the students call you directly. Obtain a deposit with preregistration. Ask the students to fill out the registration form in the catalog and send it to your address. Each teacher establishes his own registration, cancellation, and refund policies. List preferred hours in the course heading. Recognize that many students register the first day of class, or sometimes later, so don't cancel because of lack of early enrollment." Teachers must sell the course over the phone to prospective students.

The Colorado Free University tells its teachers, "All CFU teachers are independent contractors. *You* are responsible for your students, safety, and the quality of their experience." CFU pays either by the student, or by the course regardless of enrollment.

Preparation. Slide shows can add interest to travel, art, or other visual courses, and should be accompanied by instructive commentary. Other teaching vehicles include discussion groups, question-and-answer sessions (often left until the last quarter of class), and hands-on experience.

Handouts, in addition to passing along course information, are advertising which will probably reach potential future students. Doris Kennedy, who teaches a travel writing course, distributes handouts at the end of the course so students don't thumb through them while she lectures. Cara calls students a day before the first class to make contact, to be sure they have their directions, and to give them a warm feeling which reduces tension. Before each class she decides on energy level, pacing, and style, as well as the informational details.

Teaching. One-time classes often last two to eight hours, and serial classes may meet for a couple of hours once a week. Vary the pacing every half hour or so to keep people from getting bored. Stop every hour and a half for coffee or snack breaks, since many people take classes to meet other people in a semi-social setting. The way you present the material is important. In general, people will get more if they participate more. Anything that is fun is a great motivator. Each step in the course should build upon previous steps for continuity. Students will remember structured material better than fragmented items.

Always end the class with something everyone can feel good about—an accomplishment. People will fight for their self esteem more than anything else.

Many teachers address only a few short questions as they talk, saving a half hour or so after the lecture for a question-and-answer period. Others encourage open discussion. Course content determines which is most suitable. If you plan on teaching the course again, pass out a critique sheet in which students can express their feelings about the good and bad points, and things they would like to see in the future.

Run a Free School

A free school can be a one-person job, or the work of a large organization. Some schools offer general adult education courses in almost anything, while others offer themes. Nexus specializes in holistic medicine, while Conscious Connections offers mind-expansion courses. The Boulder Teachers' Catalogue offers courses in everything from travel and photography to "Allowing Love to Blossom."

Duane Fry publishes the Boulder Teachers' Catalogue himself, five times a year. He handles teachers, ads, commercial ads, layout, printing, and enrolling students for the teacher at $3 per head. "My phone number is my single most important asset," Fry says. A consistent number brings in ads, students, teachers, and other contacts year after year.

Some catalogs interview the teachers and require them to give a mini-presentation before accepting their ad. All supply teachers with written guidelines for their ads. Many catalogs include a disclaimer such as "The sole function of the BTC is to publish and distribute information concerning the courses offered by the teachers to the community. The BTC assumes no responsibility for the collection of registration, monies, course content, or teacher liabilities. Though we believe the teachers have the highest standards and integrity, we encourage all who seek enrollment in the courses offered to satisfy their needs and concerns through direct contact with the teachers."

"Use every bit of space in the catalog," Fry urges. Margins are good places for suggestions, phone numbers, interesting sayings, and bits of philosophy. Duane includes suggestions like "Dare to be changed," "Wisdom may be the only real wealth," and "Each individual lives in a unique world held together by his or her conditioning." Such thoughts not only stimulate action by the reader, but make him or her want to read the catalog more closely for additional bits of "hidden wisdom."

"I often hire a local cartoonist to do illustrations," Fry says, adding that many local writers and artists will work for free to gain exposure. He uses paste-on designs available at art stores for filler.

Commercial advertising makes up about 50 percent of the revenue of a free-school catalog. For every twenty to thirty people Fry contacts, he will sell one ad. About 25 to 30 percent of the ads turn over each issue, making his job of soliciting new advertisers a constant one.

Distribution of 25,000 to 35,000 catalogs is perhaps the trickiest of all problems. "You are competing with the local newspapers for advertisers," Fry says. "They won't deliver your catalog. Figure this out before anything else. You must spend no more than five cents per copy on distribution. Direct mail is too expensive."

Most catalogs are delivered to drop points in supermarkets, local businesses, and campuses by a local ad agency, and Duane himself delivers 5,000 copies. Fry breaks up his community into five areas, and distributes door-to-door in each area once per year. Drop points are perhaps the most cost-effective method. He takes three to four weeks to distribute an issue. All magazines are out before courses start, one month after printing.

Teachers' catalogs are a high cash-flow business. You must allocate money to produce each issue, and not spend it on other things. Fry allocates about $3,000 per issue, and reinvests as much profit as possible. To encourage new teachers, he offers to run their first ad for $30, second ad for $40, third ad for $50, and all others for $60.

It takes time for both teachers and catalogs to build up a reputation. It may be difficult to find twenty-five new teachers all at once when starting a new catalog. Advertise in the catalog for new courses and teachers.

Fry sums up by saying, "The schools which fail are often more interested in making money than teaching." He loves his job, adding philosophically, "I don't have to do this. We justify mayhem when we decide there isn't anything we have to do. When I relax and take time, people come to me."

Erik Hyypia

FREELANCE BARTENDING

The liquor business is a billion-dollar-a-year industry, and perhaps you have even thought about opening your own bar or liquor store. Then these thoughts may have been immediately dismissed, simply because the investments for starting such operations are, many times, far out of the reach of a beginner. That's why you need to know what it takes to start your own low-cost, high-profit, bartender-for-hire business. It's a business that offers you a fair share of the billion-dollar-a-year pie, without astronomical sums for a liquor license and location set-up.

How to Start

Market Research. Most people want to jump right into a business, following pure gut instinct. However, they usually find out that this can be financially deadly. Discovering whether a given market can comfortably support a business (not to mention you) is the pivotal step in establishing a lucrative bartender-for-hire business. Only after you have determined that your market area is suitable for this type of business can you capitalize on it.

Learn Bartending. If you have never worked as a professional bartender, you must learn the art. This, after all, is the crux of your new service business. The first step to mastering bartending is to start learning today. You will need to learn the basics, such as highballs, stirred, shaken, and specialty cocktails. To find out what the popular regional drinks are, you can simply ask bartenders in your area; they will tell you. You must also learn to make these drinks efficiently and correctly. The only way to become proficient in anything is with repeated practice. Set up a mock bar and stock it with empty liquor bottles filled with colored water. Practice mixing drinks behind the bar using the different bottles. Remember, speed and accuracy should be the hallmark of your service. Work to achieve this.

Finding Employment

The best way to fine tune your skills is to work as a bartender. Plus, this will give you the opportunity to meet other bartenders whom you may want to hire when your business grows. You will only need to work as a bartender part-time for a few weeks—just enough time to be familiar with what you'll be doing behind the bar.

Establish Your Business. Licenses, permits, getting a telephone number and bank account, obtaining necessary supplies, and determining a price schedule are some of the details you will need to attend to before you can even open your doors to customers. However, don't be put off by all of these details; the obstacles are minimal and the initial investment is exceptionally low. It is entirely possible to spend less than $500 for everything you will need. Here is a list of necessary items and their estimated cost:

Licenses & permits	$150
Commercial checking account	
(for check printing)	15
Business telephone number	
(use your home phone to start)	0
Answering machine	35
Buy/constructing a portable bar	200
Miscellaneous supplies	35
Stationery & business cards	50
TOTAL	$485

Fees

You will now have to set a price for your service. The charges vary widely from place to place. The secret to effective pricing is to slightly underprice your competitors, while offering better service. Finding out this information is easy enough. Look in the *Yellow Pages* under "Bartending Services" and call each place. Ask what kinds of services they offer (this should give you some idea of all the spin-off services available) and what their prices are. Charge accordingly. It is possible to charge $100 for a short afternoon party, while evening bashes make, depending on the services your client wishes to purchase, upwards of $300— plus tips.

Promotion

This is the key to getting new accounts and maintaining old ones. Use word-of-mouth advertising at first to promote your business. Also, it is imperative to actively seek free media outlets. Call newspapers and magazines to find out how your business could be featured in an article. In addition, your service is the type of business that lends itself to radio promotions. Call local radio stations and find out which ones can accommodate your budget.

Promotion also takes the form of sales documents. Develop a brochure and sales letter. Make sure that it is "client centered" and the benefits of using your service are clearly apparent. Putting all of these marketing tools to work for you will result in a profitable, quick start without spending thousands of dollars up front.

So you *can* try to open a bar or liquor store and pay megabucks for a liquor license, not to mention location set-up. Or you can get in on your piece of the billion-dollar-a-year liquor business without driving yourself heavily into debt.

For More Information

The Professional Bartending Course. A self-study program. Bartending Course, 3536 University Blvd. N., Suite 250, Jacksonville, FL 32211; $72.00 ppd.

Daniel Hall

GARDEN CONSULTING

Elizabeth Dickerson is a trained horticulturist who worked for the Burpee Seed Company and whose main job was to answer customers' questions about gardening. "I really enjoyed the challenge of the customers' varied questions," explains Elizabeth, "so I decided to advertise myself as a gardening consultant, and to set up my own business." She charges customers a one-time $50 consulting fee, and $25- to $30-an-hour teaching courses to various community groups.

Elizabeth began her business as a garden consultant. She distributed business cards and signs in local garden shops and stores announcing her services as a "horticulturist/consultant." Homeowners began to call her with various questions about their gardening needs. If anyone so desires, Elizabeth will design annual and perennial gardens plus special "theme" gardens: butterfly, colonial, fragrance, tea, moonlight, or whatever combination the homeowner decides on. In addition, she will test the soil, advise how to improve it, and give general gardening advice.

Elizabeth found that environmental concerns and recent housing trends have increased the need for her services. She says, "Many homeowners want to know how to garden organically, so their families and pets will not be exposed to potentially harmful pesticides; they are more environmentally aware of what effect these chemicals are having on our world. I show them how to grow vegetables and flowers by using natural controls."

With the increase in housing costs across the U.S., many builders are constructing smaller houses on smaller building lots. Elizabeth advises homeowners how to use medium-growing plants and shrubs that will not outgrow the property in a few years, how to economize garden space using raised beds and patio containers, how to plant for much-needed privacy, and how to create recreational space.

There is one drawback to this part of Elizabeth's business, however. "I find that I usually do such a good job of instructing, that most people opt to learn more about gardening on their own. So I seldom have repeat customers!" As a result, Elizabeth looked for other ways to expand her business, and decided to teach gardening classes. The local high school had an adult education program, and they hired her to teach a basic gardening course. Many schools will start their instructors at $15 an hour; more in the succeeding years if the course becomes a popular one. Elizabeth says, "Many of the adults enrolled in my course had prior gardening experience, so it was easy to teach them. We shared information, and it turned out to be a lot of fun. Each class will dictate what you need to teach based on students' gardening knowledge, and what they want to learn from the course."

Elizabeth also became an on-call horticulturist for a local garden shop. The shop paid her to sponsor a well attended, two-hour children's gardening workshop. Elementary-age children learned how to plant patio containers and flowers. She says, "Children love to get into dirt. Most of the parents stayed to watch, and were impressed with their children's results. The workshop was good publicity for the garden shop, and helped establish my name as a gardening expert."

Elizabeth has discovered that teaching provides a stable income for her business. She claims that people interested in starting a similar business do not need a degree in horticulture. "All a person needs is the love of growing plants, and with it an understanding of the cultural requirements of the varieties of plants used by most home gardeners and the ability to work with other people." Many adult education programs, vocational/technical schools, and community colleges can help you acquire the knowledge to teach gardening to others. She also recommends the following:

• Visit your local library. "You can find information on any gardening topic."

- Experiment with horticultural techniques. "A person who best qualifies for this kind of work most likely gardens at home, trying new varieties of plants and gardening methods."
- Volunteer to help others in their gardens. "The most valuable training you can get is not only in your own garden, but also in the gardens of families, friends, and neighbors."
- Invest in basic gardening tools, but not the most expensive. Elizabeth purchased most of what she needed at her local chain department store.

Elizabeth recommends a solid background in horticulture for anyone seriously interested in pursuing this line of work. "All this experience and education gave me the confidence to offer horticultural advice and instruction to others, yet personally I realize how much there is yet to learn. When I plan new gardens, I have the knowledge and experience that puts me ahead of an amateur, and I always try to learn as much as I can. I highly recommend that anyone thinking of going into this business do the same."

Elizabeth believes this type of business is in demand, especially in communities where avid gardeners live. "The initial investment is only about $200 (business cards, posters, basic tools). The work can be both physically and mentally challenging, but the potential rewards are there. If you persist, you can earn up to $75 an hour (during the busiest seasons). However, the intangible rewards can be even greater as you see your students become as enthusiastic about gardening as you are!"

Priscilla Y. Huff

GENEALOGY

As a child you must have heard your parents declare "Money doesn't grow on trees." Well, maybe they were wrong after all. The family tree that everyone has may indeed be the money tree you've been looking for. Genealogical research may be the means to harvest the cash crop! You can charge fees as high as $35 an hour plus a retainer fee as high as $500.

Genealogical research is the third most popular hobby in the United States, behind stamp and coin collecting. While no one is certain how many people are involved, the National Archives claims that almost 58,000 people signed in to do genealogical research in the Main Archives microfilm research area in Washington, D.C., last year. Another 24,000 used the main research room. Many more thousands—perhaps as many as 48,000—used the Microfilm Rental Program to get their information. And unknown thousands more used the eleven Archives' field offices around the country.

Unlike stamp and coin collectors who deal in merchandise, genealogists' interests are research, collection, organization, and presentation of historical information. A genealogist sells the intangible: his or her services, experience, and time. One personal quality helpful for success in the field of genealogy is curiosity. If curiosity is one of your vices or virtues, why not put it to work? Alvira Herbert of Fairfax, Virginia, did. "I realized that I didn't know as much about my family as I wanted to know," says Alvira, "and my grandchildren's questions gave me the wherewithal to find out more. When I retired I was looking for a hobby, something to do that wasn't expensive—something

I could share with my family. Genealogy was it. I'm enjoying myself and earning extra money."

Beginning

Alvira, like most genealogical researchers, started tracing family histories as a post-retirement hobby, beginning with her own family's. After the initial step of talking to relatives, scouting out the family Bible, rummaging through salvaged birth or death certificates and wills, and locating everything possible from family sources, the dedicated researcher has to broaden the search. One of the most definitive sources for outside information is the National Archives in Washington, D.C. Most researchers are astounded at the volume of information available here. Covering an entire city block, the National Archives contains 1.3 million cubic feet of historical records dating back to the Revolutionary War. But the D.C. main branch is only one of many Archives facilities throughout the country. Eleven field offices in Boston, New York, Philadelphia, Atlanta, Chicago, Kansas City, Fort Worth, Denver, Los Angeles, San Francisco, and Seattle serve people who cannot conveniently get to Washington.

Like the main Archives, each of the field offices offers research assistance and has copies of many microfilm publications, research rooms, a basic reference library, microfilm reading equipment, and document reproduction facilities. The amount of information can be confusing just by the sheer volume of it. Hence, most first-time researchers (and many highly experienced ones as well) seek assistance immediately upon starting their research. The Main Archives and most of the regional branches provide trained volunteers and staffers who offer critical genealogical research assistance which takes many forms. It may mean suggesting a research lead, or offering a word of encouragement to a stymied patron.

Another excellent source of genealogical information is available in the state of Utah. The Church of Jesus Christ of Latter-Day Saints has the largest genealogical library in the world. Because of this rich source of genealogical information, Utah also has the largest concentration of genealogists. The library's information is considered so valuable that some genealogists who specialize in areas as distant as France and Lebanon reside in Utah to be closer to their informational gold mine.

Sticking With It

If curiosity is the first quality a successful genealogical researcher must have, tenacity is the second. It often requires dogged perseverance to go through hundreds—perhaps thousands—of records before chancing upon the one magic name or the specifically desired information. Seasoned genealogical researchers advise neophytes to come prepared to spend hours in seemingly endless and fruitless searching. "Be patient. Keep looking," suggests Susan Cooper, a genealogical specialist at the main archives in Washington, D.C. "And if you get really discouraged, take a break and return after you've recouped your enthusiasm. Sooner or later you'll find what you're looking for."

Starting a Service

After completing your own family research, you might

feel ready for a bigger challenge. If through practice, experience, and exposure to the records, you believe you have become proficient at genealogical research, you may want to establish a name for yourself as a genealogical researcher. You can earn money playing detective for other people.

Once you have demonstrable results—documentable evidence of your efforts—you can apply for certification or accreditation as a bona fide genealogical researcher. Accreditation or certification programs verify your "business credentials" as a genealogist while raising the hourly fee and retainer. Two professional certification programs exist in this country: The Mormon Church in Salt Lake City, Utah, and The Board for the Certification of Genealogists in Washington, D.C., both of which award professional status to genealogists who can substantiate their expertise. Several courses of study are also available for those wanting additional information before seeking certification. Brigham Young University in Provo, Utah, offers a four-year program leading to a bachelors degree in genealogy. And The American Society of Genealogists in Arlington, Virginia, offers a sixteen-session home study course. (See below for addresses.) The course costs approximately $300, or less than $20 per lesson.

What you can expect to earn varies with your certification or accreditation, research specialty, and area of residence. Researchers living in large metropolitan areas with access to ample library data can charge more for their services than researchers living in small towns. Availability of information and experience in using that information to locate desired facts seems to determine the going rate. Small town researchers may find themselves in the $4- to $5-per-hour category for their services; metropolitan area researchers can expect to collect $25 to $35 per hour. Most genealogists charge an hourly rate in addition to a retainer fee. Retainers can run between $50 and $500, depending upon certification credentials, research specialty, information availability, and amount of information sought. Researchers can locate prospective clients through a variety of media. Alvira, for one, advertises in her local and regional newspapers in the classified ads under "Services." Other researchers use ads in genealogical magazines or magazines targeted to potential clients such as the *DAR* magazine. Still other researchers post notices in their libraries and leave pertinent information with local historical, preservationist, or genealogical societies.

The best advertising is still word of mouth. The most successful researchers find that when they do a good job for one person, that person refers them to yet another person needing research services. Their reputation and their business grow.

Getting Certified

According to John E. Dorman of the Board of Certification of Genealogists, there are approximately 500 genealogists who have been Board Certified in six sub-categories:

• Certified Genealogical Record Searchers locate specific records such as wills, deeds, and military records at the behest of their clients.

• Certified American Lineage Specialists perform line of descent research, a crucial point upon which certain membership societies (such as the National Society of the Daughters of the American Revolution) base their entrance requirements.

- Certified American Indian Lineage Specialists study tribal records of Native Americans.

- Certified Genealogists are generalists. Competent in all areas of genealogy, these researchers' knowledge on specific topics may be more limited than a specialist's. They are expected to be able to put branches of a family tree together and draw conclusions from these family links. They may be called on to testify in court when a family member contests a will.

- Certified Genealogical Lecturers speak to audiences about specific subjects concerning genealogy.

- Certified Genealogical Instructors are the teachers of the field. Though there is no formal education required to become a genealogist, it is sometimes possible to learn new skills or hone old ones through instruction.

Dorman recommends that individuals interested in learning more about genealogical research read some of the nation's leading genealogical journals including the *National Genealogical Society Quarterly*, the *New England Historic Genealogical Register*, the *American Genealogist*, and a new journal entitled *The Genealogist* (see addresses below).

Among the books Dorman recommends are "The old standby, *Genealogy as Pastime and Profession*, by the father of genealogy, D.L. Jacobus, and *Genealogical Research Methods and Sources* (two volumes), published by the American Society of Genealogists."

Two national associations offer guidance to budding genealogists. They can help neophytes get started and can suggest answers for the "What do I do now—I've tried everything I can think of" dilemmas.

For More Information

For Certification:
The Board for Certification of Genealogists, P.O. Box 19165, Washington, D.C. 20036; or P.O. Box 2022, Columbia Rd N.W., Apt. 107, Washington, D.C. 20009.

Home Study Course:
The National Genealogical Society, 4527 17th Street, N., Arlington, VA 22207; for $300. According to Marion Beasley, librarian, "the course puts you through the paces doing your own genealogical research."

Trade Journals:
National Genealogical Society Quarterly, published by The National Genealogical Society, 4527 17th Street N., Arlington, VA 22207.

New England Historic Genealogical Register, published by The New England Historical Society, 101 Newbury St., Boston, MA 02116.

American Genealogist, 128 Mossasoit Drive, Warwick, RI 02888.

The Genealogist, published by The Association for Promotion of Scholarship in Genealogy, P.O. Box 1058, Rockefeller Center Station, New York, NY 10185.

Journal of Genealogy, Box 31097, Omaha, NE 68131.

Books:
Genealogy as Pastime and Profession, by D.L. Jacobus, Genealogy Publishing Co., 111 Water St., Baltimore, MD 21202; $7.50.

Genealogical Research Methods and Sources, published by American Society of Genealogists, P.O. Box 4970, Washington, D.C. 20008.

How You Can Trace Your Family Roots. E.A. Morgan Publishing Co., P.O. Box 1375, Huntington, NY 11743-1375; $8.

Associations:

American Society of Genealogists, P.O. Box 4970, Washington, D.C. 20008.

Association of Professional Genealogists, Box 11601, Salt Lake City, UT 84147. Annual membership: $35.

National Genealogical Society, 4527 17th I Street N., Arlington, VA 22207. Annual membership: $30.

Ellen Paul

LIMOUSINE SERVICE

Everybody wants to go in style—to weddings, concerts, business meetings, even funerals. And what better way to go than in a fully-equipped, chauffeur-driven limousine? More and more people are riding in style to propose marriage, celebrate an anniversary, close a business deal, or go to the theater. Limo providers are cashing in, charging $40 to $125 an hour for each car.

Cities and towns lacking limousine service may be fertile ground for starting a part-time limo business if there is a proven demand. Prospective operators can take heart that the market is broad, that it isn't just the well-heeled who are renting limos. "High schoolers are among my best customers," says Wayne Winner, owner of a limousine service in Pennsylvania. "What the kids do is pool their money together at prom time so they can have a night to remember. And one reason business has been good is that a lot of ordinary people are discovering that hiring a limousine isn't as expensive as they think. I charge $85 for the first two hours and $26 for each additional hour. So if three couples are going to a prom, it comes out to about $15 or $20 a person. A lot of my clients hire cars for long trips. The total cost, when divided among six passengers, can often beat the air fare. The people can go in all that luxury."

Corporate clients frequently use Wayne's service to transport visiting executives to and from the local airport. Promoters generally hire a car to ferry entertainers to local engagements. Although he's been in business for fourteen years, Wayne's enterprise is still growing and total sales are increasing an average of $10,000 a year. Wayne started his limousine service with a five-passenger Lincoln sedan. "It went over so well that people wanted to rent my private car, a Chevrolet Monte Carlo, so we used both," says Wayne.

Over the years Wayne continued to trade up as profits warranted, and today he has three late model Cadillac stretch limos that offer such extras as TVs, VCRs, stereos, and bars. The sticker price of a new stretch limo begins at around $35,000, but many used models sell for under $10,000.

Steps to Start-Up

Setting up a limousine business often requires the approval of government regulators. "In most states you have to file an application with a controlling agency to prove there is a need for the service," Wayne says. "You'll need a lawyer and you may have to get affidavits. If no one raises any objections, there's a good chance the agency will approve a license if all conditions are met."

One of the conditions is adequate insurance, and it isn't

cheap. "Anytime you haul passengers for hire, you're a bigger-than-normal risk," Wayne explains. "So your liability insurance is going to be 300 to 400 percent more than it would be for a regular car policy."

Wayne says persons interested in starting a limousine service should first conduct a market survey to make sure the income levels and demand are high enough to support one. The next step is to buy a good used limo—unless you have a lot of money to spend—then work your way up from there. Advertising is extremely important to educate the public about the services offered, so it's essential to set money aside for that, too. Because appearance and reliability are musts, the vehicles will need plenty of attention. "I contract with a mechanic to provide twenty-four-hour service," says Wayne. "At the first sign of a problem, I take the car in."

To reduce the cost of hired chauffeurs, Wayne does as much driving as he can. One of his sons also lends a hand, and his wife, Mary, assists with bookkeeping and other chores.

"If you put in the hours and do your homework, and if there's a definite need for your service, you can succeed," Wayne says. "I now service eight counties, and I plan to get two more stretch limos in the near future."

Mike Cummings

MOBILE DISC JOCKEY

Imagine a job that involves going to parties, playing music, and talking with people who have their hearts set on having a good time. Sound good? Well, that's exactly what a typical work day is like for Robert Lindquist. Robert operates The Musical Roadshow, a successful mobile DJ service in western New York State.

The mobile DJ business, like all businesses that provide services, is part of the fastest-growing segment of our country's economy. "And what makes it so great for someone starting out," says Robert, "is that it takes no special skills and a very small investment to start a profitable mobile DJ business." According to Robert, mobile DJs often get their training by working in radio or clubs. Others become mobile DJs because they are obsessed with music and enjoy being in front of people.

On-the-Road Training

Robert began over twenty-five years ago with a couple of friends. Their jobs consisted of playing for church youth groups, high school sock hops, and birthday parties. "Occasionally we would get paid, but for the most part it was just fun," says Robert. This early experience paid off. Today, operating Musical Roadshow mobile disc jockey service is what Robert does. "Although I occasionally play pubs and lounges, our specialty is private parties," says Robert. Well over two-thirds of his bookings are wedding receptions. Other events are birthdays, anniversaries, Bar Mitzvahs, graduations, family reunions, dinner dances, class reunions, fund raisers, high school dances, sock hops, retirements, and holiday parties.

Four Success Components

A successful mobile DJ business is made up of four

components: the electronic equipment, love for music, an understanding of what people want when they hire a mobile DJ, and a desire to succeed. Robert explains that someone beginning a mobile DJ service can spend a little or a lot on equipment. The basic outfit includes two manual turntables, one audio mixer/preamplifier (control board), one main power amplifier, two loud-speaker systems, a microphone, and a pair of headphones. In addition, some DJs elect to include a cassette deck, reel-to-reel tape deck, or CD (compact disc) player in place of one or both turntables. To maintain better control of the quality of the sound, an equalizer may be employed. Also, speakers on stands help the sound reach the back of the crowd. A mirrored ball, light show, or other theatrical effects might be included.

Most mobile DJs create their first set-up with a combination of components from a variety of sources, usually a combination of rented or purchased used professional and home stereo equipment. "It would be great if you could purchase professional equipment from the start. It's manufactured to hold up under the rough use that it will see on the road. But most people can't afford the $3,500 to $4,000 that a professional set-up might run them," says Robert.

Robert recommends that you take a hard look at your budget and divide it up in the following way: Spend no more than 60 percent of your total start-up capital on equipment. Of that 60 percent, plan to spend about one-third on turntables, one-third on your board and amplifier, and the final one-third on speakers, headphones, and a good quality mike. Regardless of the size of your budget, keep that 60 percent figure in mind. You'll need the remaining 40 percent for records (or CDs) and supplies, advertising, and possible emergencies. Plan your system carefully; buy only what you need.

One advantage that mobile DJs have over live bands is that mobile DJs are able to play a variety of music, from heavy metal to country with a bunny hop thrown in for good measure. Rarely would a live band be able to provide the flexibility in music that a mobile DJ can provide. But how do you decide what music to take along to a job when there are potentially millions of choices? Successful mobile DJs like Robert offer this advice: "If you are buying more than a few records, talk to the manager about a discount. Many are happy for the extra business a mobile DJ brings and may be willing to shave a percentage off the price for you."

Besides the right equipment and a ready supply of hot tunes, a DJ must know what his clients want. "A mobile DJ is expected to be professional," says Robert. "There are five areas where a DJ might have a problem: volume, music, control, preparation, and appearance." Here are his tips for these potential career wreckers:

Volume. The most frequent complaint made by un-happy customers is that the DJ played too loud or too soft. When you've been hired to provide background music, keep it soft, but make sure it's loud enough so that everyone can hear it. Listen to the guests. If they say it's too loud, turn it down. If they want it louder, crank it up.

Music. The same is true of music. Many DJs get into big trouble when they don't play what the client requested, especially when it's on the play list. Never prejudge a group. If they request a polka, play one. If they want the bunny hop, hokey-pokey, or stroll, play it! Don't make it your mission to introduce the crowd to your own "Pick Hits of the Week." Play what's established and familiar. Play the hits past and present. When in doubt . . . leave it out!

Control. No matter what type of job you're booked for, you are expected to do more than just play music. A good DJ is a total entertainment package. This is not to say that you should sing, tell jokes, dance, lip sync, or try to amuse the crowd by conversing with a rubber chicken, but you do need to get involved and *take control.* The DJ is responsible for getting everybody into the spirit of the party. If you want to succeed, don't hide behind your table. Talk with the guests. Find out what they want and then give it to them!

Preparation. Failure to prepare yourself mentally and physically will ultimately cause you to become disorganized and lose control. Before each job, clear your mind and think through what you're going to do. Psych-up by convincing yourself that you're going to do a good job and have fun. Don't think of it as work. Work can mean stress, and stress leads to burn-out. For peace of mind, make a checklist so that you have a quick way of making sure that you have all your music and equipment. When you get to the gig, seek out your client and go over any last-minute details. Find out what is expected of you before you start to play.

Appearance. The last "horror story" told by people who claim "I'll never hire a DJ again" is: "He came to my wedding reception in a T-shirt and jeans. I was so embarrassed." Unbelievable as it may seem, it still happens. The fact is, people do judge a book by its cover, so always dress neatly. Some DJs go all out and buy or rent tuxedos. For others, who like to change their appearance from job to job, a sport jacket and tie work well. Don't brand yourself an "unprofessional slob" by wearing anything less. Needless to say, this rule is not universal, as a sport jacket or tuxedo would not be fitting for a Halloween party, outdoor picnic, or similar, more casual event. For these occasions, ask your client ahead of time what is appropriate.

Finally, if you want to make it as a mobile DJ, it is necessary to have the strong desire to succeed and the willingness to make your own opportunities. The demand for mobile DJs is steadily growing. With a few pieces of equipment, an awareness of music sources, an understanding of what your clients want and a willingness to work and dream, you too can be part of this exciting field.

For More Information

Spinnin' 2000 by Robert A. Lindquist and Dennis E. Hampson. L.A. Publishing Co., P.O. Box 43, East Rochester, NY 14445-0043.

Clare S. Dygert

OUTDOOR GUIDE

If you have a love for the outdoors and a concern for the environment, you might parlay these passions into an exciting business. Cari Taylor-Carlson of Milwaukee did. She is beginning the fifth year of her company, Tripping

Lightly, which provides guides, destinations, food, and equipment for backpacking, biking, canoeing, and other outdoor adventure trips.

Cari has always enjoyed backpacking with friends and is quite knowledgeable about the environment. This knowledge earned her a staff position for The Girl Scouts National Center West camp. Later, when she served on the staff of a women's camp, a number of the participants urged her to guide a trip for them. "I decided there was no time like the present," Cari says. "I started the first trip with myself as guide, using my own tent and utensils, so I didn't have to invest in any equipment in the beginning." Her main start-up cost was a flyer she sent out.

The First Steps

Cari started out slowly, part-time. "The first year I guided only two trips," she says. Today, however, Tripping Lightly employs thirteen guides besides Cari. She has gradually added other tents and equipment, and this year she is offering twenty-eight different trips, plus a day hike every Saturday. The trips include such impressive itineraries as snorkling in the Virgin Islands, exploring the Florida Everglades, rafting the Salmon River, and more local safaris such as biking in Wisconsin's beautiful Door County and canoeing the lower Wisconsin River. Cari selects her sites and excursions either because she has enjoyed having the experience herself or because she has a reliable guide who is an expert on that terrain. "I never take a group on a trip that I haven't already done myself, or can provide a guide who has done extensive tripping in that area," Cari says. She feels it's important to know what she's getting people into. There are enough surprises in weather and nature as it is.

Selecting Other Guides

Many of the guides who work for Tripping Lightly were originally clients, so Cari had plenty of opportunity during various trips to see how they responded to crisis, pressure, and getting along with other people before she put them on the payroll. Cari has been fortunate to find people with special expertise and credentials: Chris Schwartz is an ornithologist who specializes in bird watching trips; Phil Sigglekow, who guides canoe trips, is a canoe manufacturer and a seminar leader in canoeing skills; Bill Volkert is a naturalist with the Department of Natural Resources at the Horicon marsh; Nancy Frank is Director of the Wildlife Arc and shares her expertise in both wildlife and natural history. With a little effort you should be able to find similar people in your community who enjoy sharing their knowledge and skill.

Cari sub-contracts some of her trips to other outdoor guide companies that she knows to be reliable and certified—trips such as a walking tour in England, or a llama-packing trip in California. Her recommendations often turn out to be reciprocal, as those companies may then contract with her to provide Wisconsin adventures for their clients.

Proper Frame of Mind

The "mind-set" of the guide is important, Cari says. You, or the other people who guide for you, must be up-beat, positive, and encouraging. Not all the experiences on an outdoor trip are going to be pleasant. There will be times when people are too hot, too cold, tired, hungry, dirty, or stung by insects, or the words or actions of campmates will get to them. Sometimes it requires an infinite amount of patience and compassion on the part of the guide because people can get "real crabby when they're cold and hungry," says Cari.

The challenge has always been to deliver what Cari feels is the bottom line for Tripping Lightly: that the clients have an enjoyable time they can look back on in pleasure despite whatever temporary discomforts occur. "It's real interesting," Cari says. "You become an observer of people, and people do rise to the occasion." It is a rare trip on which the participants do not become very close-knit and experience a deep level of friendship and companionship, even if there may initially be some abrasive moments along the way.

Basic Equipment

Cari uses two-person Urika tents which are lightweight and durable. She also keeps camp stoves and cooking utensils as lightweight as possible. For the most part, she does not use freeze-dried food on the trail, though she does resort to mixes. Main courses are built around sturdy foods such as pasta, rice, bulgar, and lentils. She might make a noodle casserole, fettucini, or spaghetti. Other favorites are pilaf, curries, and stroganoff. She likes to provide a satisfying dessert like mousse or cheese cake, which are easily produced from mixes. There are few vegetables and no meat (which takes care of refrigeration problems as well as vegetarian clients). Muffins and pancakes help to make filling meals and are also easily prepared from prepackaged portions that only need water added. Cari supplements this menu with dried fruits.

Cari carries a well-stocked, extensive first-aid kit and a rope. Clients are expected to furnish their own personal gear such as flashlights, sleeping bags, skis, snorkling gear, and backpacks.

Planning the Trips

Groups range from eight to twenty people, the criteria being based on the activity. "We usually never take more than eight people camping," Cari explains. "But it's possible to have a group of twenty when we go on the English walking tour or other events that include meals and lodging at an established site." As an example she mentions the four Wellness Weekends on which indoor sleeping and eating accommodations are provided. Likewise, the snorkling trip to the Virgin Islands includes beach cottages for sleeping and a main lodge for dining. Often, inns or hotels in the area will be eager to cooperate with you.

Cari has found it helpful to her clients to offer a pre-trip schedule of meetings to help answer their questions and give them any additional information they need concerning what gear they will need, the routes and terrain that will be covered. and what difficulties might be expected. She does this because it is not easy to cover everything in a brochure. The pre-trip meetings are also an opportunity for the people involved to meet their tripmates.

Cari also provides an equipment list and other printed information three weeks prior to the trip. She advertises her trips in four categories: Women's Trips, Coed Trips, Educational Trips, and International Trips. She does not take children. "I love children, but adults are less responsibility," she says.

Liability and Costs

Cari has never had any serious accidents or deaths during her years of guiding. A few cuts, insect bites, and stomach aches are about all she has had to deal with, but liability insurance is crucial. "You wouldn't dare operate without it," she says, and it is expensive. It is the single most costly item in running her business, but there is no alternative. Cari carries a half-million dollars' worth of insurance.

Her other major expense is for printing and mailings to advertise the business. The response to such mailings are usually about 3 percent, according to marketing experts. Cari says, however, that 10 percent of the people who receive her brochures actually take a trip. She credits a carefully targeted mailing list for this success rate. "We only mail to groups we know have a leaning toward outdoor activities," she says.

Cari and her employees also get lots of free publicity for Tripping Lightly by giving talks, speeches, and presentations to all sorts of groups. Even though the presentation might be on a topic such as preserving the environment, Tripping Lightly is bound to get mentioned, and Cari always has brochures to hand out. She has also used T-shirts for promotion.

Other expenses, which you may not need at the outset, have been the purchase of a computer, artwork for the brochures, and an accountant.

What to Charge

The fees charged for each trip are determined by the fixed expenses plus whatever special costs the trip might require and the required profit then added. "We just punch it all into the computer," Cari says. She requires that half the cost of the trip be paid upon registration (of which $50 is non-refundable). The balance is required three weeks prior to the trip. Refunds are given only if she receives notification three weeks prior to the trip. She also sets registration deadlines for some of the trips and charges an additional $25 processing fee for late registrations since they demand extra effort.

Cari has been astonished at the pleasure the business end of her enterprise has given her. Like most entrepreneurs, Cari says that you have to love what you are doing to make a success of it, and the biggest reward of Tripping Lightly is "to do something I love—and I do love it, every aspect of it." Originally she thought the pleasure would come mostly from the outdoor part. She has found, however, that the business part is "a challenge but comes close to being as exciting as the actual guiding." Watching her business grow through her efforts has been a tremendous satisfaction.

Cari's final bit of advice to people who would like to follow in her tracks is, "I'm careful to see that I don't repeat the same trips all the time. I would get stale." You have to keep your own romance and joy with the trips or you won't be able to share the sparkle and enthusiasm that make a good trip. Ultimately, it is that sharing that makes a trip a special and unforgettable experience for your clients.

Barbara Vroman

PICKUP PROFITS

If you own a pickup truck, you're in luck because it can start delivering cold cash. Here are a few ways to make that hauler bring in income for you in just about any part of the country. They are only suggestions; they've worked for others, but don't restrict yourself to these. Look around and you may find some that are better.

Hauling Landscape Rock and Wood

In many housing developments, homeowners are stuck with landscaping walls and forms made up of cement block. But many of these homeowners would prefer something more distinctive, if it could be delivered to the site. So here's where you and your truck come into the landscaping picture: wherever there's running water (beaches, rivers, even small creeks) there are smooth stones, often of amazing beauty and diversity, and equally attractive driftwood. Collect them, then bring your pickup—loaded to the gunwales with selected rocks and wood—into a higher-priced, rapidly sprouting tract, and show your wares to both home builders and contractors. One rock-seller gets $150 to $200 per load.

Motorized Hayrides

Kids in the suburbs may have heard of hayrides, but how many of them will ever join in a pastoral, moonlit tour of nearby country roads? Not many, but a lot of them—and their parents—would pay well for the chance. This is an income idea for which you need do no actual hustling: contact church and community youth group officials and tell them what you have in mind. Hay's cheap, the overhead is negligible, and you'll be pleasantly surprised at the reaction. This has become a regular weekend job for several West Coast entrepreneurs. Youth groups are always looking for wholesome ways for their little charges to spend Saturday evening; they'll supply refreshments and do all the tiresome organization. And getting $50 or more for taking a pleasant drive in the country ain't exactly hay.

Fireplace Maintenance Service

After Joe Homeowner burns the wood you (or someone else) sold him, you can haul away the ashes for him. Customers are easy to find, since this is probably the most avoided household chore there is. Ashes collect fast, and people are quick to delegate the sooty task to an enterprising odd-jobber and his half-ton. In many cases, they'll happily sign on for once-a-month service through winter. All you need for this chore is a wide shovel and a waste can.

Appliance Repair Shop Delivery

Have you ever watched somebody groan, sweat, and curse while trying to wrestle a power mower or television into the trunk of his car? You can be sure he'd much rather have someone else—you—do the job with a suitable vehicle: your half-ton. But he can't stand that extra $10 for a service call. All you have to do is set up a pick up and delivery service for one-man-shop repairmen, most of whom would rather stay in their little shops and tinker than shuttle from customer to shop all day. Incidentally, it's almost a reflex for customers to dispense healthy tips to eager-beaver deliverers—a "gravy" addition to the fee from the repairman.

Hay Supply

In most suburban areas are neighborhoods zoned light agricultural, which almost always means horses, not vegetable gardens. Junior equestrians have their own horses, usually kept in small backyard paddocks. Those pampered hayburners are your in: as the hayman, you become as indispensable as the milkman or the mailman. Actual ranches, of course, have their hay shipped in by the twenty-ton load. But the ever-present suburbanite horseman must drive miles for his steed's staff of life, and then hoist those heavy bales in and out of the trunk of his compact car every week or so. So you get in your truck and canvass these one-horse "ranches" and offer to provide a weekly hay delivery service. If you're planning to become the fodder mogul for, say, twenty customers with twenty-five horses, buy a twelve-ton load (the price of hay fluctuates with the season), jerry-rig a shed to cover it, and distribute three-quarter-ton per week to the score of horses. You can easily charge $10 per bale, more if hay's scarce, and clear a tidy $80 to $100 for an afternoon's work one day each week.

Little League Chauffeur

Here's a proven income ploy which involves no paperwork on your part, save for a monthly trip to the bank. An unemployed West Coast plumber contacted the managers of the six Little League teams in his small town and asked them to inform the youthful sluggers' parents that, for 50¢ per head, per team, per event, he would transport the kids en masse to meetings, practices, and league games (a Little League team, complete with equipment and batboy, fits easily into the bed of a half-ton). By the way, the kids will be your best salesmen if part of the deal is a stop at the local hamburger haven after games.

Economy Towing Service

What does Joe Motorist do when he's stuck on a muddy stretch of lonesome road? He beats it to the nearest gas station pay phone, calls the nearest neighborhood towing service—and gets stuck for $50. You, your half-ton pickup, and a standard-length tow chain can do the job for half the price and still make a comfortable profit. In order to catch the benighted motorist's attention before the fast-buck towing serviceman (who has a $16,000 rig to pay for), you merely spend an afternoon pasting notices in out-of-the-way phone booths. With emergency road calls averaging ten million per year in the U.S., and a good number of those being simple soft-shoulder pull-outs and empty gas tanks, you can bet that your phone (and your wallet) will get a real workout. Don't worry about your hauler; it can yank a passenger car out of anything short of quicksand with negligible wear and tear to either vehicle. A couple of sandbags in the truck's bed insure traction under wet conditions, and don't forget that gallon of gas. Don't sell yourself short; a stranded driver is a captive audience and will be happy to pay $20 to $30 to have wheels again.

Shopping Center Delivery

Anywhere there's a modern shopping complex offering lower prices and centralized location, there's also a group of older, smaller, neighborhood businesses that must offer better service to avoid going under. One way the little grocery, pharmacy, and liquor store can compete is by delivering. This way the little guy can keep his old customers and gain new ones: housewives stuck without a car all week, oldsters too tired to hoof it to the nearest shopper's "mall," and others who prefer personalized service to slightly lower prices. Many small butchers, bakers, and grocers can't afford full-time delivery service. So what you do is contact members of a neighborhood shopping area as a group and farm yourself and your hauler out to as many of them as are interested. Work out a schedule that gives each of them one or two "delivery days"—and everybody profits.

RÉSUMÉ WRITING

Before anyone embarks on a job search—whether he is a veteran in the work force or a recent college graduate—he'll need a résumé. Since résumés play such an important role in a job hunt, they demand special attention. Writing, designing (choosing paper, typeface, and format), and producing them may be a job that you have a knack for doing. You may have heard about résumé-writing services, but never knew how they alone could sustain a business. This service, though, is something that is always in demand, can easily branch out into other forms of typing services, and requires little overhead and start-up capital.

There are several different types of résumés, chronological and functional being the most popular. The chronological résumé is the traditional detailed format most often used by beginners and those who have not had many job changes. For someone with a diverse or broken job history, the functional résumé may prove best. This concentrates the most pertinent information in a useful length. Some of the other types are analytical, creative (used only by those in "creative" professions), Harvard, narrative (similar to a letter), and the professional résumé used by professional people such as physicians and professors.

There are other types of résumés used for purposes other than seeking employment. Political candidates have very brief résumés that are long on personal information and political accomplishments and short on occupational background. Campaign literature resembles creative and functional résumés. After-dinner speakers also provide detailed résumés to the person who will introduce them at a meeting. These résumés most resemble professional résumés.

If your client has something to hide, such as a jail term, talk with him or her about the advantages and disadvantages of including a reference to it in the résumé. In a chronological résumé that lists everything, it would be lying to omit it. But the client can get his foot in a new employer's door without lying by stressing such things as skills in a résumé, instead of arranging the jobs in the order he held them. The subheadings for this type of résumé would be "Sales Experience" or "Skills" or "Truck Driving Experience"; it should not list everything the job seeker did since high school.

You will discover that you and your customers prefer one or two basic formats. Most people will allow you to format the résumé for them. However, others may show you exactly how they want the formatting done. In the end, you will want to use something that looks good on one page. If one or two lines run over to the next page, you will have to either reformat or rewrite it to make it look appealing on one page. Always proofread a résumé. Check for typos, grammar, and meaning.

To write a résumé, you will have to know what one looks like. Check out books on résumé writing at the library, or buy your own at the local bookstore. Keep samples of anonymous résumés to refer to (don't show one customer another's résumé). A résumé requires the job seeker's name, address, and phone number at the top of the page. You can also write "résumé" at the top of the page, but it is redundant and often a space waster. You should list work experience and education in sections under the subheadings "Experience" or "Education." It is also important to list achievements in reverse chronological order. Your client must also decide whether he or she wants to include a career objective, and have his or her work experience come before their education or vice versa.

You should allow résumé clients to call you at night because some can't call during the day with the employer hovering nearby. Treat all résumés like rush jobs. Anyone who is out of work hates the waiting game. Since you are at home, you can receive the information "after work hours," finish it after supper, and have it ready the next morning for the job seeker to take to an interview. Request that they stop by a little early in case there is anything you need to change before their job interview.

Supplies

If you don't have one, buy a typewriter or word processor plus a few office supplies. Set a price for each service—both typing and writing—and you're ready for business.

A home computer with simple word processor software and a letter-quality printer are available for as low as $800. The high end is as much as $3,000 for a top-quality home computer, including all the software and hardware. The printer *must* be letter-quality; a dot-matrix printer simply will not do for résumés.

If you plan on using a typewriter, keep in mind that many people prefer an IBM or a similar typewriter with changeable type balls. You can purchase a good portable typewriter for about $200. Once business begins to pick up you can think about upgrading. When using a typewriter, be sure to keep the keys or balls clean and use only a single-strike ribbon. Typewriter repair costs upwards of $55. If possible, get the best equipment at the beginning, because portable typewriters and those designated for "college" or "home" use will not stand up to the volume of work a business puts out.

If you do not have a computer or word processor, you can use a plain paper copier, which you can get for under $1,000. You can charge as much as 25¢ for single copies, or for dozens of copies you might want to go down to as little as 5¢, providing it covers the cost of running the machine. Keep copiers clean and in good repair. Dust, streaks, and light or dark impressions on copies simply will not do. When you are using machinery or electronics on a daily basis, it pays to know a few basic maintenance techniques.

Essential office supplies consist of the following: plain white bond paper (20 or 25 weight), inexpensive copy paper for the copy original or rough drafts, colored bond résumé paper when you provide all the copies, #10 envelopes, receipt books, file folders, paper clips, and at least three extra typewriter or printer ribbons (always stock up on ribbons). In addition, you will need typewriter cleaners, useful for cleaning computer keys and platen. You can obtain bond résumé paper at the office supply store. You can find the other supplies at discount stores. Many people will prefer plain bond paper to the neutrally colored special résumé paper. Whatever paper you do choose to use should measure 8½" x 11". Never use paper that measures 8½" x 14" unless a client requests it, because it is unwieldy.

What to Charge

What you charge depends on the going rate in your market and what part of the country you live in. You should find out what other résumé services in neighboring areas charge before setting your price. Some charge a set rate, some by the page (from one-page to three-page résumés), and others charge by the hour. You might charge $5 for typing, for example, except in large cities like Los Angeles where typing alone runs $25 an hour. In many other cities some services charge from $30 to $60 or more for writing a résumé.

Where no one else has this service, charge $5 to $10 to attract job seekers of all economic means. If you must charge more later, you can, but it is easier to go up in prices than to go down after you have gained the reputation of being expensive.

Branching Out

You don't have to be a great writer to run this business, but you may be asked to write a cover letter or customized letter to a specific company to accompany the résumé. Sometimes the client knows what he or she wants to say in the cover letter and can provide specific information, but doesn't want to do the writing. Some job seekers ask you not only to write a résumé and cover letter, but to help them fill out their application, especially if it is a detailed, difficult Civil Service application. This represents extra income.

Once your business begins to thrive you can add other typing services. Areas to consider are brochures, flyers, newsletters, and college students' reports and thesis papers. If you just want to stick to résumés, that's okay too. No matter what you decide to do, by starting a résumé service you are providing a needed service to your community and earning a living from a business that is yours.

For More Information

The Résumé Catalog: 200 Damn Good Examples by Yana Parker. Ten Speed Press, P.O. Box 7123, Berkeley, CA 94707; $10.95.

Résumés That Work by Tom Cowan. New American Library, 1633 Broadway, New York, NY 10019.

Better Résumés for College Graduates and *Better Résumés for Sales & Marketing Personnel* by Adele Lewis. Barron's Educational Series, Inc., 113 Crossways Pk. Dr., Woodbury, NY 11797.

Sandra G. Holland

TUTORING

Deborah Schadler and her friend Karen Horoschak were often frustrated in their years of public school teaching in not being able to give individual help to those students they knew could benefit from one-to-one tutoring. With their class loads and sizes, they simply did not have the time. Debbie and Karen retired from teaching to raise their children, but still tutored friends' children as a favor. When Debbie began to tutor almost everyday, she decided to find out if she "officially" could go into business, with Karen to help her.

Debbie conducts her business from her home in an addition she had specially built onto her house for that purpose. Its spacious, attractive, and unclassroom-like atmosphere helps students feel relaxed and ready to learn. Students in kindergarten to grade twelve from five surrounding school districts are tutored throughout the year. "We begin with a few students in September," says Debbie, "and by March we are packed with students who need help to pass a course or work toward a scholarship." Debbie and Karen get very few students through newspaper advertising, even in the special educational issues. Most of their referrals are "by word of mouth." Parents will make the first initial contact, then Debbie and Karen will contact the district and the student's teacher and guidance counselor.

Working with Teachers

Debbie and Karen strive to work with the school district and teachers, but they have found the biggest problem in schools is the lack of communication between the teacher, student, and parent. Debbie and Karen have compiled a simple, quick checklist for the teacher to fill out weekly so Debbie and Karen can monitor a student's progress in the subject for which he or she is being tutored. This checklist has been valuable in bridging this communication gap. With such support, students realize Debbie and Karen really care about their progress. The students, in turn, try harder to improve.

Parent involvement after the first initial contact is one of support. "Sometimes," Debbie says, "we have to separate the parent from the student. We have to 'educate' the parent into stressing the positive, not the negative." After assurance from the parents that they will give positive encouragement, Debbie and Karen begin tutoring.

Tutoring elementary students is different from tutoring junior and senior high school students. With an elementary student Debbie never tutors the student without the recommendation from the teacher. Promoting a good self-image for this age student is one of the most important factors Debbie and Karen stress. They urge the student's teacher to follow through on this concept. For this reason, Debbie and Karen like to have elementary students referred to them at as early a grade level as possible. Debbie says they find that by fourth grade many students are already "locked-in" to a certain concept of themselves.

Also with the elementary child, Debbie and Karen will use totally different texts from the classroom, so the material will be new and interesting for the child. This makes it easier to keep up the child's interest in learning. Debbie and Karen will work on more specific areas such as comprehension where needed by the elementary school student.

With the secondary student, after the initial request for tutoring by the parent, Debbie or Karen will contact the teacher, then report back to the parent as to what areas the student needs help. Debbie says the objective for students of this age is usually to pass a particular course. They want the student to "get through" that course on a report card basis.

Debbie and Karen do not only tutor students who are having difficulty. They also tutor honor students who are competing for scholarships, preparing for SATs, and some who are attending college. When students who are having difficulty in a subject hear that such "top" students are being tutored by Debbie and Karen, they don't feel so "dumb." It makes them realize all students need some help at sometime in their educational years. They see Debbie and Karen's tutoring service is for all students who might need to improve in one or more areas.

What to Charge

Since most of the students are from middle-class families, Debbie and Karen try to make their service affordable. They charge $12 to $15 an hour. They charge this fee based on the cancellation rate, the cost of materials, and the cost of maintenance of the equipment. Debbie says, "The biggest cost is having to buy books from the same companies as school districts which do not, as a rule, shop around for the best prices." This results in expensive materials.

There have been some surprising sidelines to Debbie's and Karen's business. Debbie teaches at the local high school's adult evening school, and both Debbie and Karen teach homebound students who are recuperating from illness, accident, or an operation. But a surprise for Debbie was the number of requests from parents of Debbie's students who said they had never quite grasped a subject and would like some extra help. Debbie schedules these adult students to come in the daytime, before the school students begin to come in the afternoon at 3 P.M.

Debbie was at first afraid the material for adults would be too juvenile, but found most publishing houses to have good educational material at the adult level. For a fee of $100, Debbie will give the adult student a complete battery of tests to determine the adult's level. Included in the fee are the materials and tutoring by Debbie or Karen until the person completes the course. Debbie says she is more a "resource person" as the materials are independent study, self-help courses. Debbie says, "It's up to them to learn. I figure they're adults, and they will learn what they need to learn."

Another branch of Debbie's business was the establishment of study groups. Students come with others at designated times to do homework, research, and prepare for tests. If they need help, Debbie and Karen are there to help them. Debbie does not yet charge for this study time, but as the number of students increases, she may.

More Sidelines

Local businesses have approached Debbie and Karen to provide still another business sideline. One business had Debbie teach a grammar "refresher" course to fourteen men who were promoted to managerial positions. The company president wanted the men to be able to use the correct business English and grammar to "fit" their new positions. Still another local business asked Debbie to help the large number of Hispanic employees become better acquainted with our language.

The most exciting sideline of Debbie's business is the summer program she and Karen direct. "This is *our* program!" Debbie says. "We do not have to follow any other teacher's plans. There are no limits to the creativity we can put into the sessions," which they call the "Summer Reading Maintenance Program." There are incentives and rewards for the students as they work on reading skills so they will not fall behind in the summer months. Then Debbie and Karen hold a party at the end of summer for all their students who attended this program.

For More Information

The Tutor Book by Marian Arkin and Barbara Shollar. Longman, Inc., 95 Church St., White Plains, NY 10601. $14.95.

Tutoring: A Guide for Success by Patrica S. Koskinen and Robert M. Wilson. Teachers College Press, P.O. Box 1540, Hagerstown, MD 21741. $5.95.

Priscilla Y. Huff

Part Six:

4 PART-TIME REPAIR & MAINTENANCE BUSINESSES

AQUARIUM MAINTENANCE

"They say I'm into a new-age enterprise," says John Giacchi. "But to me, it's something I love doing. It's like a hobby, and it makes a profit." John runs John's Aquarium Maintenance. During any given month, he visits approximately 100 fish tank locations in doctors' waiting rooms, building lobbies, offices, restaurants, cocktail lounges, private residences and, most frequently, dentists' offices who feel a fish tank in the waiting room can relax uptight patients. "It's my responsibility to make the fish tank look as good as possible and to keep the fish healthy," says John.

On an average day, John tends to as many as ten fish tanks or as few as three. Many are oversized and require as long as three hours each to be thoroughly cleaned. In some respects, John is not unlike a doctor. He often receives emergency calls that run the gamut from sick fish; broken filters, pumps, or heaters; to accidental water spillage. Leakage doesn't occur often, but when it does, says John, it can be an absolute disaster. There was the time, for example, when an exterminator serviced the restaurant of a client and accidentally split the seam on a 175-gallon fish tank that sat behind the bar. "All of the water, some 250 pounds of gravel, and about fifty African cichlids were flopping about on the floor," remembers John. Fortunately, there were two other fish tanks in the restaurant and John was able to scoop up the fish and toss them into the undamaged tanks. The rest of the cleanup was a matter of collecting the spilled gravel and decorations and supplying a new tank.

Another of John's favorite "emergency" stories goes back to a New Year's Eve several years ago when he received a call from the non-client manager of a cocktail lounge who told him that a customer had poured a glass of vodka into a 150-gallon fish tank. To replace the water, it was necessary for John to stand on the bar where the celebrating crowd made a game of using him as a target for straws, napkins, maraschino cherries, and a variety of other loose materials. As John describes it, "While they were throwing things at me, I had to empty the tank, put fresh water into it, adjust the temperature, and ensure that the water was clear while balancing myself on the bar." The story has a happy ending: the crowd gave John a standing ovation. He rescued the fish and he gained a new client.

John's job includes changing the water, cleaning the tank and filter, replacing charcoal, and eliminating algae. He also repairs or replaces tank motors, pumps and heater elements, and checks on the well-being of the fish. John maintains that experience is the only way to recognize the difference between a healthy and an ailing fish. On occasion, he has healed sick fish with antibiotics. But of everything he does, John says the most difficult task is to service a tank installed into a wall at an awkwardly high level.

John travels from client to client in a large service vehicle resembling a van that he bought used for $7,000 plus a $150 charge for painting the name of his service on both sides of the truck. The vehicle is kept stocked with approximately $500 worth of cleaning equipment and supplies, including hoses, siphons, buckets, and spare parts for tank accessories. John also pays $1,500 a year for general liability insurance geared to a small service business, workman's compensation, and vehicle insurance, which is a legal requirement in New Jersey. His major expense is driving back and forth to his many clients. John estimates that he spends approximately $300 per month on gasoline. Charges for the monthly aquarium maintenance visits range from as little as $40 to as much as $150 for an oversized tank located at a site that requires lengthy travel time. John also feeds fish on a regular basis for vacationing clients; there is a special charge for this service. And he has noticed that "the owners don't mind paying from seven to fifteen dollars a visit because they know the fish are in good hands." John has never asked clients to sign a contract, relying instead on verbal agreements. "I never thought about the need for a contract during the first three or four years I was in business," he says. "Clients have since asked me about it, and I explain that I don't think a signed agreement is necessary. If I do a miserable job, chances are you will never see me again. But no one has ever told me I've done a poor job."

John told everyone he knew about his business. Then one day John received a call from the owner of a nearby tavern who wanted him to clean his fish tank. He had heard about John's service from one of John's friends. Since then, the venture has continued to expand, always by word-of-mouth recommendations. For the first year or two, John used his own automobile and a supply of buckets, hoses, and sponges that can be purchased at discount stores for under $100. A business telephone and an answering machine required a $200 expenditure. The cost of professionally printed business cards was roughly $75.

Fish tank maintenance is a service that is needed everywhere in the country. And John believes that with the right personal characteristics and some preliminary self-study, it can be a venture for anyone. As John says, "Buy a fish tank and practice. Read as much as possible about tropical fish and their tank environment. And try to locate a friendly tropical fish store owner whom you can watch in action and who will answer a lot of questions. If you wish, take a job in a tropical fish store to gain hands-on experience."

Most important, John stresses, a would-be aquarium maintenance worker must be an animal lover, either self- or academically educated, patient, and calm. "I work with piranhas, moray eels, an alligator called the 'camen,' and with lion fish that are extremely poisonous. I handle them with respect," he says.

Mildred Jailer

AUTO STRIPING

Auto-related businesses are among today's most promis-ing money-making ventures. Unfortunately, many of these businesses require special training, equipment, and a large investment of time and money to get them started. How-ever, there is one professional area of expertise in the auto industry that entrepreneurs often overlook. It's a business that many people are capable of training themselves in after receiving a minimal amount of instruction, and one that they can start on very limited funds.

When automobile manufacturers first started applying stripes and graphics to their vehicles, they did so with paint. When technology enabled auto makers to create automotive striping out of vinyl, they quickly switched to this less expensive and more durable product. The idea soon caught on, and it wasn't too long before people began to specialize in the design and installation of vinyl stripes and graphics for automobiles. Auto detailers presented their products and skills to the new car dealers, who immediately took advantage of what they were offered. Usually, a new car dealer can have a stripe applied by an auto detailer—like you, for example—for less money, and with a more professional job and a better product. The dealer is able to offer his customer a custom-designed stripe or graphic so the customer doesn't have to settle for what happens to be "available."

Putting a pinstripe on a car may sound like a difficult job, but with practice and determination, you'll quickly master the knack of it. When Troy Robison first got into the striping business a little over six years ago, his boss told him that he would have a one-week training period. It should have been called a one-week *practice* period. After the basic instruction, he learned the rest on-the-job, until he developed the proper skill and learned all of the tricks. Many of the skills needed to do this type of work are intuitive. For example, an installer can "feel" whether or not the tape is in the proper place better than he can see it.

Guidelines for Striping a Vehicle

First, thoroughly clean the area of the vehicle where you will place the stripe. Use some type of wax and grease remover such as Prep-sol, Acry-sol, or TFX cleaner. When the area is clean, make a continuous wipe from one end of the car to the other with a clean, soft, dry cloth. The continuous wipe is important because if you lift the rag half way down the side of the car, you'll leave a deposit of dirt on it.

After you thoroughly clean the vehicle, begin laying

the stripe by tacking it down at one end of the car. Unroll a few feet of the tape at a time and apply each section as you go. When you have an entire side done, press the tape down to set it against the surface of the vehicle. Do this gently at first to prevent the tape from sliding around, then go over it to secure it.

Use a very sharp razor blade to make the cuts at the ends of the stripe, at the doors, and anywhere else on the surface where it might be necessary (door handles, mirrors, door locks, etc.). Make these cuts about one-eighth of an inch from the door edges. Do not wrap the ends of the tape around the door edges because they have a tendency to peel off. This is because you cannot clean all the dirt out of these recesses, so the tape will not adhere properly. Remove the waste material and the carrier (the plastic covering on the vinyl) as you make the cuts along the side of the vehicle.

The vinyl stripes will actually set on the finish of the car like paint. The stripes eventually harden so they will not peel off, but instead chip off like paint. In addition, even when the stripe itself is removed, the adhesive will often remain.

Pricing

The prices for installing an accent stripe, or pinstripe, vary in different parts of the country. In some places, installers give them away to promote other accessories. In other parts of the country, dealers are paying as much as $25 for them. A price range of between $10 and $15 would be a good place to start, until you settle on what the going rate is in your area.

Pricing for stripes, other than accent stripes, and graphics is usually figured as follows: two-and-a-half or three times your material cost for the stripe, more if the job required some detail work or elaborate craftsmanship. However, never under-price your work. If you do, the dealers will get in the habit of paying too little. Then, when you finally realize that you are worth more than you are charging, they will balk at paying the higher prices.

Being dependable is very important to the success of your business. Let the dealer know on which days of the week you will call on him, and then get into a regular routine. Stick with it, even if you are getting little or no work from him. If the dealer sees that you can give him the best service, even if he's not giving you any work, you will eventually get the account. Do not call on more dealers than you can handle. This will only cause headaches for everyone involved and will endanger all of your accounts, especially if you have competition. It's advisable to start by contacting a small number of dealers whom you can provide with good service.

There are as many used car dealers as there are new car dealers, but for the most part you are better off avoiding them. Usually, a used car dealer will not want to pay a fair price for a striping job, and will frequently try to give you demeaning tasks such as covering up rust spots, striping over old stripes, or removing old stripes. One such dealer talked the author into putting a four-inch wide stripe over a hole in the hood of a car. Also, removing old stripes is something you should never do if you can avoid it. The older the vehicle, the more trouble you will have getting the old stripes off.

What You Need to Start

Since one of the keys to running a successful striping

business is regularly calling on new car dealerships, you will need some sort of dependable transportation. The vehicle should get good gas mileage and be roomy enough to carry all of your supplies. A car will work fine for starters, but a small station wagon would be better, and a light truck or van is best. Whatever vehicle you choose will serve as your shop, warehouse, and transportation. You can use your home as a base of operations as well as an office, reducing overhead.

To be readily accessible to your customers, use an answering machine so they will be able to contact you even when you're out on a job. If you are only going to be working in one city, it's a very good idea to invest in a beeper, or paging system. If you are working in more than one city or town, and they are a few miles apart, the beeper is unnecessary and more of a hindrance than a help.

Do not rush out and buy a few hundred dollars' worth of striping tape and then immediately start calling on new car dealers. Instead, buy only two or three rolls of 5/16, double-pin tape and practice for a few days on friends' and relatives' cars. Get the hang of it first, so when you approach a dealership and ask for the owner or new car sales manager, you'll know what you're doing.

You can buy striping tape at any auto parts store, and at department stores such as K-Mart and Wal-Mart. There are several manufacturers of automotive striping vinyl in the U.S. Sharpline Converting and Universal Products produce a top-quality tape, and will happily send you catalogues and ordering information.

A 5/16 double-pinstripe is considered the standard accent. This is a 1/8-inch stripe with a parallel 1/16-inch stripe and a 1/8-inch void separating them. However, this is not the only size tape you will need. Dozens of colors are available in sizes ranging from 1/16-inch to a few feet in width. To start with, you should have two or three dozen colors of 5/16 double-pin, twenty or thirty colors each of 1/4-inch solid, 1/2-inch solid, and 7/8-inch solid, along with about a dozen colors of 2-inch solid striping.

The material listed above will probably cost between $600 and $1,000. You could get by with fewer materials in the beginning, but sooner or later you will need them and more. Some manufacturers and suppliers will extend credit for up to thirty days, so it is possible to start this business with only a few dollars.

Other supplies you will need to buy with money from your own pocket will be invoices, and some sort of book-keeping system to keep track of your accounts. In the beginning, you will probably have to deal on a cash-only basis with your customers. After you get the business going, however, you may want to extend credit, as some dealers will prefer this method. Ideally, what you will end up with is some accounts who charge, but others who will continue to pay by the job. This way, you will have a continuous cash flow to take care of miscellaneous expenses.

Troy Robison

HANDYMAN; ODD JOBS

Maintaining and beautifying a home can be an endless and expensive struggle. Walls and window trim are forever in need of paint; shrubs and bushes require yearly trimming; and light carpentry and yard work are seasonal chores that face every homeowner. Weekends, which were once reserved for home improvements, are now a time to shop for necessities or leisure activities. Many people who work forty-hour weeks are not inclined to pick up a paint brush or seal their driveway. Usually, people hire an expensive professional to do the job.

The double-income family is less burdened by professional prices, but is most likely sensitive about giving their hard-earned money away. This is especially true if there is a possibility of getting the job done for a considerably lesser amount. In addition, senior citizens often own homes that are in need of repair. The high prices of a professional can restrict a cost-conscious elderly person from having work done, especially when certain necessary home improvements are small and do not require a professional.

An inexpensive odd job service is an alternative to all these problems. There is a definite need for such a service and an odd jobs venture, if executed with vigor and integrity, can be the start of a very profitable business. Opportunities for household odd jobs exist wherever there are homes and homeowners, rich or poor, who must contend with the upkeep of their property.

You need not take on jobs which require sophisticated equipment. However, as you develop capital, you might invest in a used lawn mower or electric hedge clipper. These investments will enable you to expand your services to weekly yard work.

Getting Started

In order to begin a home-oriented odd jobs business, one must be in close proximity to people who own homes.

The type of homes are relatively unimportant, but most jobs come from middle-class homeowners who need home improvements. Operations may begin at any time, but the best time to actually start is in the spring after the last of the snow has melted. With the advent of spring, the homeowner becomes much more conscious of his home's appearance, especially considering the state of a home after a long winter. Snow and freezing weather often tear off branches and leaves, and many yards need thorough clean-ups. Yard clean-ups which are done in both fall and early spring can yield, depending on the size of the yard and the amount of debris, $100 to $300 per yard. The only equipment you'll really need for this job is a rake and some plastic garbage bags.

A large yard clean-up usually takes four people about three hours to complete. If you are able to secure a clean-up for $200, your income for the job could be quite substantial. A $200 job requiring three employees to work for three hours generates about $53 dollars an hour for you. Your cost of labor is $12 an hour or $36 for the entire job. If you subtract $8 for advertising expenses, your final earnings could be $160 or $53 per hour.

A professional landscaper, on the other hand, would charge about $50 to $75 more than the prices quoted here. By using the *Yellow Pages* as a resource, call landscapers and pose questions to them as if you were a potential customer in order to determine what a professional charges for a job. When you have learned the prices they charge, undercut their prices.

In the beginning you will not have the sophisticated machinery of a professional, but by being innovative, you can save yourself time and money. Search your attic for old army blankets or quilts. Lay them on the grass and rake the piles of leaves onto them. When you want to shift the pile on to the street, collect the corners and lift.

Selecting Services

Selecting which services you want to offer your community is a simple task. Any specific skills you have should be emphasized in your advertisements. Don't worry if you do not possess any special skills. Most household repairs are simple enough to be done by almost anyone. Moving furniture, raking leaves, and painting are basically unskilled tasks which you can find yourself hired to do time and again.

Certain jobs, however, should be left for professionals. Doing electrical work or plumbing can be extremely dangerous unless you are qualified and licensed. Test and see what your community needs. Look through the *Yellow Pages* to see which services have the largest number of businesses. You may find an inordinate number of professional painters, indicating that many people had homes in need of painting. This method of determining what your community needs is by no means foolproof, but it can give you a semi-accurate "feel" for your market. As you work in your community, you will begin to become more aware of your customers' needs.

Pricing

Pricing is perhaps the hardest part of running an odd jobs business. It is impossible to put a specific price on services that vary from job to job. For example, you might be hired to move a refrigerator. However, every refrigerator is a different size, and no two refrigerators have to be

moved the same distance. Certain moving procedures require more workers or have more obstacles.
Here are two ways to charge your customers:

- Determine the price of the job by estimating time, labor costs, traveling time, and so forth. Then give the customer a flat rate. An example of a flat rate would be $200 for a yard clean-up. Charging a flat rate means that no matter how slowly or quickly you finished a job, you would get the agreed-upon price.

- Offer a wage rate. A wage rate is an agreed-upon dollar-per-hour-per-worker rate. An example of a wage rate would be charging a customer $10 an hour per worker. If you are at a job with two other employees, the customer would be charged $30 per hour. You will usually use a wage rate when a customer needs a considerable amount of work done and it is difficult to determine individual prices for all the necessary tasks.

You can also contract out your employees to other businesses in the community. The beauty of such a practice is that you will make about $4 to $5/hour per contracted employee.

Pricing jobs is a variable issue and you can accommodate your prices according to income levels and specific needs of a customer. If an elderly couple needs two guys to help around the house for a week, perhaps you can charge them $7 to $8 an hour instead of your standard $10 or $11 per hour. You can determine your own pricing formulas that will work best in your community.

Supplies

Do not supply any materials for customers unless you are explicitly asked to do so. In most cases, you can be

innovative enough to make do with the customer's resources. For example, if you are painting outdoor lawn
furniture, you can often find newspapers stacked in the
customer's garage. Newspapers make a suitable drop
cloth, and you save the customer the expense of having to
go out and buy one.

Certain materials, however, need to be bought. Paint,
for example, is a necessary purchase. In such instances, buy
the paint and give the customer the receipt; or add a
surcharge to the price of the paint for having to buy it
yourself. Giving the customer the freedom of being able to
buy materials works out well because the ultimate cost of
the job can be defrayed.

Advertising

Advertising may be achieved by printing up flyers, placing ads in newspapers, or both. If you plan to advertise with
flyers, design or draw a flyer which can be run off by a copy
machine. Perhaps your advertising can consist merely of
flyers written in calligraphy accompanied by drawings. Professionally printed flyers or advertisements with elaborate
designs may look sharp, but the process is costly and it can
give a high-priced impression. Remember, the low cost of
your services is what will attract customers. If your advertising projects an image of high-priced services, you may very
well scare off a large portion of your clientele.

The flyer should be a conservative, to the point, one-
page advertisement. Using catchy phrases is not bad, but
the flyer should definitely include some of the services you
wish to offer, and a phone number where you can be
reached. A one-page flyer, if copied at a reproduction store

or a local library, can cost as little as 10¢ a copy. If you have access to a copy machine, you can make hundreds of flyers for free.

Many households have both spouses employed in the work force and food shopping is done on the weekends. Find out when the local shopping centers experience the greatest volume of shoppers. Hand out flyers at this time to get the greatest exposure. You'll find that many times, while handing out flyers, you will often receive on-the-spot phone numbers or invitations to come over and estimate a job.

Flyer campaigns can be successful, but you will probably solicit the majority of your customers through newspaper ads. Most communities have a weekly local paper which is basically a gossip column and a medium for local businesses to advertise. Advertise in such a paper by placing a 1" x 1" advertisement; it'll cost about $8. Also consider advertising in the Sunday edition of a daily newspaper with a slightly smaller version of the same advertisement; this ad may run about $12 per week.

Quality Service

We cannot emphasize enough the importance of giving quality service. The only aspect of your business that should differentiate you from a professional is your price. Take pride in your work and always be polite, attentive, and professional. Project an image that says that you are reliable and caring. You will often have customers rehiring you to do jobs because they are so impressed with the quality of your initial effort. These customers are more concerned with the care you put into your work, rather than the particular skill needed to do the job.

In one such case, a customer hired an odd job crew to weed her property weekly. The crew was very meticulous about their work and, after four weeks of weeding her property, the customer decided to let them stain her patio decks. The decks surrounded her entire house and required four people to work a full week. The job brought in over $2,500 in revenue.

You Can Clean Up

A twenty-year-old ran such a business for three summers, and two out of the three years offered odd job services. In those two summers or eight months of work, he earned enough money to finance his entire undergraduate college education, a semester studying abroad, a three-month European summer vacation, a car, a computer, and a portfolio of stocks, bonds, and an IRA.

Dedicating weekends or two hours a night can often bring in significant amounts of extra income. Your operation will not be as sophisticated or as detailed as a full-time venture, but that by no means restricts the opportunities. The beauty of running an odd jobs business is that an investment of as little as $8 a week can be enough to get the business off the ground. Odd jobs, in essence, sell labor and you are the labor.

Eric Davis

LOT CLEANING

Randall was happy to be home from college and have some time off. But now what? He couldn't just sit around for the next three months before school started again, so he decided to find a way to make some extra money—quick. He checked the classifieds and looked at the supermarket bulletin boards, but everything was minimum wage. He didn't want to spend the summer in a fast food restaurant. Then he got the idea to create his own job and at his own price. He would do lot clean ups.

Randall's hometown is situated in an area that is not heavily developed, and has plenty of vacant lots. Usually these lots are owned by people that live out of town. These owners can be cited by the fire department if the lots become a fire hazard by collecting debris and tumble weeds. They are subject to a fine if the lot is not cleared within ten days.

A notice is posted on the lot and the owner is sent a registered letter notifying them of the fire hazard. If they don't reply within the allotted time, the job of cleaning the lot is made available, and whoever wants to can bid on the job at the city hall. The cost is paid by the city and comes out of the property owners' taxes. Randall got many of these jobs by being the low bidder. Yet the income was still excellent.

To get additional work, Randall photocopied dozens of one-sheet flyers to distribute house to house. He offered to clear weeds away from fences so residents could pass the fire inspection. He also offered to remove unsightly garbage and trash to increase the beauty of the neighborhood and city and enhance property value. He was in business.

Tools of the Trade

Randall's initial investment in equipment was minimal. "I went out and got a rake, shovel and plastic bags,"

Randall says. "I already had a pickup truck." His start up was less than $100. Randall also made a homemade "drag" out of a heavy piece of frame metal (you could use old springs from a box-spring mattress). He uses it to drag from the back of his pickup to rake the lot and help clear the debris. He learned this from the way baseball fields are dragged.

Lucrative Lots

Randall began by cleaning lots for a few extra dollars for a couple of weeks, but when he saw how many property owners of underdeveloped property had been cited, he knew there was good money to be made. He found that the highest fees come from the large undeveloped lots. Depending on the size and how much work has to be done, he earns anywhere from $250 on up. With homeowners he would offer a flat rate or ask if they preferred to pay by the hour. "It's whatever they feel more comfortable doing, but I always make out pretty good," says Randall.

Randall intended to do this work for just one summer, but it turned out to be such a lucrative venture that he decided to continue with the business each year and expand. "Next year I'll be better prepared and maybe go into removing stumps and tree trimming," he says.

Even if you don't live in the wide open spaces, there are always lots to be cleared. Someone has got to do it and they are getting paid for it, so why shouldn't it be you?

Jo Ann M. Unger

INDEX